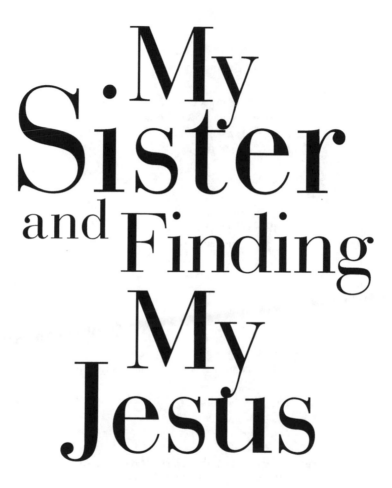

My Sister and Finding My Jesus

ERICKA JAMES

WESTBOW
PRESS®
A DIVISION OF THOMAS NELSON
& ZONDERVAN

WestBow Press books may be ordered through booksellers or by contacting:

WestBow Press
A Division of Thomas Nelson & Zondervan
1663 Liberty Drive
Bloomington, IN 47403
www.westbowpress.com
844-714-3454

Scripture quotations are taken from The Holy Bible, New International Version®, NIV® Copyright © 1973, 1978, 1984, 2011 by Biblica, Inc.® Used by permission. All rights reserved worldwide.

ISBN: 978-1-6642-9745-6 (sc)
ISBN: 978-1-6642-9746-3 (hc)
ISBN: 978-1-6642-9744-9 (e)

Library of Congress Control Number: 2023906463

Print information available on the last page.

WestBow Press rev. date: 04/26/2023

Contents

Dedication

To my children. You have and will always be my favorite people and my most important ministry. I hope you know that there was never anything to me more rewarding than being your mom. My dreams came true each time God gave me you. Remember that you are worth more than all the gold.

About the Author

For first time Author, Ericka James, this has been a long journey that started eleven years ago when she felt led to tell her children the story of her sister. After falling in love with Jesus nineteen years ago she is still very aware that He is the same God as the one she read about. She is a single mama raising four children starting from age nine to sixteen years old. They live in a small town where you can walk to the local diner for breakfast and cows line the fence on the way out to the big city. Her favorite hobby is definitely taking a nap, gardening, serving God, and watching her kids do their passion. Which usually means cheering from the stands at baseball, volleyball or basketball games or watching the school's One Act play that her oldest daughter is a part of. Her home is a place where kids and teens feel safe to gather to hang out and tag along for church.

My Life Now

*Let the redeemed of the Lord tell their story - those
he redeemed from the hand of the foe.
Psalm 107:2 NIV*

A replica of my little sister is what she is. Her laugh. That big toothy smile. The way she loves you big! As I carried her in my womb, I prayed she would be like my sister. I desired a reminder. Someone I could look at and do better by. But before she came into my life, I lost two babies, suffering two miscarriages at three months. I just prayed. Somehow, I also knew that God would keep His promise to me. I prayed for my first daughter, her name means "The Lord Answers "and He did. When I was on the hunt for a name for her, I came across her name and knew it was what I needed for her. Just one small way to glorify God for the promise He gave me. God gave me a daily reminder of my sister, and there is a great peace in that. I get to see a glimpse of her every day with my daughter. Oh, especially my youngest daughter. She has her hair, smile, dimple, and body frame. Though this reminder brings a bit of sadness sometimes, I feel so loved by God that He made two of my girls so much in her image. I believe sorrow and love coexist with grief, which never really goes away. I am thankful for this scripture: "Sorrow is better than laughter, for sadness has a refining influence on us" Ecclesiastes 7:3 NLT. I wholeheartedly believe that the sorrow that came from my sister's death brought me a refinement that I might have not otherwise experienced.

The fact that my oldest and youngest remind me so much of my sister is beautiful. Many people from my youth love to remind me of how all my kiddo s give them a glimpse of her. It's beautiful to me. When a loved one leaves this earth. You don't go on like they never existed. In fact, sometimes you cling to how your children remind you of your family. I daydream about what she would be like or how our lives and relationship might have been. Would she be like I hoped and dreamed? Would we have a great relationship? How would the holidays look? Would we live near each other? I miss her. It's crazy how you can dream up a whole life for someone you have lost, especially when they had their whole lives to live out. I watch sisters with just a tiny bit of envy. I'm happy for them to have one another, but I wish that I had mine here still. She made life fun and shined so brightly that you felt good in her presence. It is obvious to me that I am missing out on something, so I dream about what we would be like together now. What would her life be like? I even sometimes ask myself what I think she would do in some instances in my life. Some decisions are made with her in mind. Especially giving out extra kindness.

For as long as I can remember I have been telling my own girls to be kind to one another. Well, all four of my kids. Sharing with them a little bit about my sister helps. They call and know her as Aunt S. In fact there is a picture of her on a bookshelf in one of their rooms, wearing her big happy smile with loose, white curls around her face. It was taken at Chuck E Cheese during a birthday party. Of course they don't know the details, but they know that she **lived** and that I miss her every day. So, I do my best to teach them that our time here on earth is limited even though it can be too short. I want them to be there for each other and not to waste time being petty and unloving. They should be able to see the world in a bigger picture than just the present problem they are facing. Unfortunately we let the little things bother us or let them get us self-centered. Then regret comes. Regret and I are friends in a sad way. I don't like her much, but she is nice enough to come around so sometimes I wallow. Not for long, but long enough that my heart sinks. And long enough that it helps me make better decisions.

To this day, I still have a hard time answering when someone asks me how many siblings I have. How can I include her and still avoid divulging all the details? It's difficult to leave it at, she was killed when she was eleven and I was eighteen. Her time may have been short, but let's be honest: she was on earth for practically twelve years. I can't leave her out. She's my baby sister. It's still a bit exhausting, even after twenty plus years. The listener's reactions are the hardest part of telling even a small bit of her story - of my story. I have realized that leaving her out of the equation is easier for the stranger or new friend to swallow. It's like a punch in the gut still; all the air leaves my body. They can't believe it; honestly sometimes I can't believe it. Not me, not my sister. It's not like young people *never* die. Maybe by nature we assume life is great for everyone or at least that they haven't suffered great tragedy. It's not that we can't believe it but that we face the reality of what such a great loss suggests and the sadness it brings to life. But after so much loss, I hope that I have been a light, or a testimony to the beauty of life after such a tragedy. I pray that like me and so many others who have found life in God's true and holy Word, one can choose to not be buried with pain and sorrow that may come our way. There is peace in knowing God.

When you go through something like a loved one being murdered—not just death but the horrific and the brutal act of someone being murdered—life is dark and lonely. Especially when you don't have anything in life to sustain you. My sweet sister was murdered just five days before her twelfth birthday. Five days before we would celebrate with balloons, cake, ice cream and presents. That all-time tradition so many of us celebrate, especially us mothers. Every birthday is a great milestone in my book. I love celebrating birthdays, and yes, I'm the crazy mom who must be sure her kids feel extra special on their birthdays. It's like that for me in part because she was taken five days before the day the Lord gave her to us. But I do it for my friends and my kids' teachers. If I love you, and I love a lot of people, then I plan on making sure to give you something sweet on your birthday. I want to recognize you and thank God He gave us you! To me children are a gift from God, but they don't necessarily belong to us, they belong to the Lord, and He trusts us to care for them here on earth. Because life is so precious, I find great joy in celebrating birthdays! At my sister's memorial service we released lots of balloons in honor of her birthday. We stood on the sidelines of the football field she cheered on. I was there to say a few words to the community and thank them for all of the generosity. To thank them for the help in searching for her and my youngest brother. So many of her friends were there, so many people that loved her. Everyone there was better for having known my sister. She was certainly worth celebrating and I hated the fact that I will never have one more birthday with her.

Life has been very different since her death in nineteen ninety-seven. Our family was already in a dismembered state. Often I wonder what our lives would be like had she not been killed. I wonder if our family would have continued in its meager existence and if we would have remained close until each of us moved on to big jobs or college.

I'll never know what may have been, because in that moment, when her short life ended our paths all took different routes. Both of my brothers went their own ways. My Irish twin and I shared a similar path, broken relationships, and poor choices but my baby brother had his own battle to fight, and it was fierce. He has a story to tell and I believe that he was spared on that awful day because he has something to give to the world. Even if it's his own family he creates. His life is a miracle.

The next seven years my life was a big fat mess. Even if it didn't look like it on the outside. Internally I was dead as well. Many times my heart would whisper to me that I needed something more, almost like my heart felt the emptiness of not having a relationship with God. I was disobedient and adulterous; enslaved to the idea that I was a victim. Unfortunately I kept thinking that I needed to find a spouse to help make me feel less alone. Thinking back to those days there was a constant feeling of embarrassment and hopelessness. But the truth is I didn't know what I was doing, or what I should do. Certainly there were no real wants or desires my heart truly longed for. My world felt overwhelmingly lonely and scary. I had both hands up in the air, screaming, "What do I do?" I had no plan or guidance and was not sure what to do with my life. I was merely existing.

Fast forward a few years in my life and I pray my sister would be proud. Or at least happy for me. Not that I have any accomplishments but because I found her Jesus, the Savior with whom she dances with now. I found Him the hard way, but in doing so I found freedom and peace. I found *life*. When I was carrying my youngest daughter in the womb, I had a conversation with God. We agreed that if it was another girl I would give her one of my sister's names. It was always on my heart to honor my sister and fulfill my heart's desire. It was hard to name this little girl; really hard. I knew she was my last baby so it was like my last hurrah and I wanted to be sure to get it right.

Even though she was not planned like her three siblings, she was still a dream come true. What a long road it has been to get here. From two miscarriages to praising God for a fourth baby, God knew what my heart desired. My kids aren't replacements for what went wrong with my family; not even like a do-over, but they are like a dream come true. Looking at my four little ones, I feel immense love and gratitude realizing that I could have chosen a different path with sad bitter results. I know that I prayed for each and every single one of them and they are all here. My life has been redeemed. But that wouldn't have been had I not found Jesus.

If I hadn't sat down and read the Bible there is a great chance I may still be walking in a circle around my huge mountain I called dealing with life. I realize now that I just didn't know what to do or how to cope with my great losses. What to pray for or seek. I was a lost soul. It's what I know now about who I am that freed me. How and why Jesus died for me. Nothing in life makes me feel more complete or gives me more peace than Jesus. My heart and soul have felt that way since I read the Bible and found all the words that God had for me. And you too. That he was waiting for me to find. Waiting for you to find. Life no longer feels like a burden to carry around the next seventy years or so. It became a blessing to me once I decided to follow Jesus. Have you heard that song- The lyrics go, "I have decided to follow Jesus, no turning back, no turning back." It sends my heart upwards to the heavens. I love that song. The words are spot on for someone who carried all of these burdens walking around a mountain of a mess. I think of my life then as this motocross looking road that is filled with potholes and rocks that I needed an ATV to travel on and yet I was just aimlessly running it barefoot. Incurring all of these slashes on my feet that represented the scars on my heart. Unfortunately my lack of self-awareness kept me making the same decisions. But my heart started to heal once I saw that my path was clearer with Jesus. No ATV needed, just newfound hope. In fact, maybe Jesus was the ATV?

Before I read the Bible, I may not have shown it, but I had become fearful of the world. In fact, before May two thousand four, I thought it would be easier to die. To drive off a bridge. Just plummet to the concrete. So many times I thought of ending my life. It would have been perfect for me had I not woken up each morning. The idea of not enduring each day to sit and reflect or think about everything was tempting. What I was doing wrong or about my future. About the fact that my sister would never walk into the door smiling at me or annoying me. Truthfully living life without her here on earth with me seemed hopeless. I was so scared. Lonely. My best friends from high school would be shocked to see me write this. They thought I was so strong. Yet, they wouldn't know that I was dying on the inside. After my sister's murder, my mom in prison and my family rocked to the core, I wanted to die. On the inside my soul was screaming at the world. Screaming at myself. I was afraid to live and I felt hopeless. Life seemed a little meaningless. A lot hopeless actually. But believe it or not I did stand tall. Proud. As though that is what God wanted me to do.

The Christian foundation that my children have is so much better than mine. Rarely did the word Jesus, or was scripture shared in our home. I heard the song "Jesus Loves Me" but it had no real meaning to me other than a cute little song babies sing. No doubt I believed in the Creator of the Universe, but I didn't walk with Him or know Him. There was no relationship. Certainly I knew nothing about the power of God. Growing up I know that we prayed before big holiday meals but there were no talks with my family of God. We didn't discuss loving others, serving God, or spreading the Good News. We didn't do devotions together and discuss God. So when I say I didn't know God, I really do mean that. Once you hear the Good News it becomes a really different way to view life. It is Good News.

One summer while swimming in the pool, my two oldest kids were playing a game. The oldest said, "Ok, I'll take all the Christians who don't know God, and you take all the other ones." What a profound and haunting notion! I should have asked out loud "What's Mommy?" to see where they viewed me but I wanted to listen in and see what happened next. There are so many people who claim, "I am a Christian," but they don't really know or walk with God. Perhaps some of them were like me. You know God, or our Creator, is up there, but that's about it. There are some that go to church, lead small groups of people, go to everything the church has, but I wonder if they casually talk with God or pray to Him? I say that because they still gossip, and drink like they have never met Jesus. For me, I wanted to change for him. All of a sudden I had something to live for. An aspiration. I don't think about how great it is to have Him in my corner because I can keep on sinning and be forgiven. That seems to demoralize the greatness of what Jesus did for me. There is a very big difference between believing in God with just a surface level awareness and actually having Him deep down in your soul. Acknowledging His presence in the world pales in comparison to being led by the Holy Spirit and taking actual ownership of being a disciple of Christ. Committing your life to living like it. In my youth I believed that there was a God, but that was about it. There is so much more to that story. To live out your life with Jesus. Since my belief and knowledge of God was minimal to me it seemed acceptable that all this chaos was for a reason. A bigger plan from the man upstairs, right? Why else would He let my baby sister be murdered? What never crossed my mind is that God doesn't cause harm or pain. He isn't the author of sorrow. When I hear people say after someone has died that God needed another angel … I cringe. After knowing God for real now I do not see God as a puppet master that likes to see what havoc He can wreak. He's not in the game of taking loved ones from us so that we can live our lives in deep sadness or anger. Or so that He can watch us bring ourselves out of the sadness. And he doesn't need another Angel. He wants to be with us no doubt. He wants us to spread the Good News and to be representatives for Christ. For sure He has given each of us a purpose to live out. My past view portrayed that God was simply up there handing out things just because He can. But I don't believe that anymore. I get overwhelmed now with all the goodness that is in my life. My full life. When in a conversation with friends we would joke that I definitely suffered enough bad for my whole lifetime. That I need no more sorrow. Sometimes we measure misfortune and suffering as something we deserved or earned from our own sinful nature or our parents. Truth is I've even contemplated whether any more suffering will befall me the rest of my life. Even thinking about it makes me feel ill. But it is life. Life isn't only good or only bad or even only a little of both. Life is life. Those aren't the terms I think about anymore. Every day is just a crawl to do the best I remember to do. Yes, I said remember because I sometimes fail to do so. Even with all of my hardships you would think I know a better way to see things. In more difficult times, I pray more; when nothing is going on, I am just grateful. There's no doubt that we can get frustrated in life about where we are or where we wish we could be. Undoubtedly we forget to be grateful that we are still doing life, that we still have the opportunity to serve, give and love. Do life a little bigger than mediocre. Whatever happens, it should be counted all joy. Like James says in the Bible, "Consider it pure joy, my brothers and sisters, whenever you face trials of many kinds, because you know that testing your faith produces perseverance." James 1:2

Now, the devil - he is playing a different game. He loves death. He loves destroying your life and burying you in sin that leads to feeling condemnation. The Devil wants to lead you to stay stagnant in his grips.

It took me a long time to get past a few things that came with losing her. Anger, hopelessness, fear, and wandering lostness. Death is a jolt of reality. It forces you to face thoughts that you can't keep on the far back burner or ignore any longer. Unfortunately you are reminded that life is really fragile. And an absolute beautiful miracle. There is also that sense of urgency to those who have never thought death could come close to them. Don't get me wrong, I can't wait to get to heaven and see God and hug Jesus and dance with my sister; however, I want to live on earth as though everything is eternally bound.

My lifetime friend, whom I love like a sister, lost one of her brothers who served in the Marine Corps. He didn't die serving in the war; he died of something else. Truth is, it doesn't matter how or what he died from. He died. He is gone from this earth and it hurts. Just like my sister's funeral, I could not stop my tears. I remember holding my three-month-old baby in my arms when the family came in and I locked eyes with my best friend and my heart fell to the ground. She looked at me with this all-knowing look, and my eyes blurred over and I had to breathe. I knew exactly what she felt. I felt it too, again. Truthfully I broke knowing that she felt exactly what I did years before. My baby sibling was gone. It is heartbreaking to lose a sibling. He had a heart of gold, a funny guy with big brown piercing eyes. An apple of his Father's eye. One of a family of seven siblings. After hearing the news of his death while collecting my thoughts, I wondered if he knew Christ the way I did. Had he accepted Jesus as his Lord and Savior? Said those words with his mouth and his heart? Will I see him in heaven? If you read through the Bible, I mean really read it, God doesn't give you a bunch of rules to keep, per se. When you read the words in red, the words of our Savior, do you hear the call to accept Jesus Christ as **YOUR** Lord and Savior? Do you believe that He is the Messiah? Did you know Him? The one who was born in a dirty horse trough and lived for thirty something years and died a brutal death on the cross. Have you accepted Him? He is the One who was rejected by His own people, was spat upon and forced to wear a crown of thorns, and who boldly asked God to forgive those bringing about His death. Did you accept that One - my Jesus? I believe that when you do you give Him the chance to change you, save you, and free you. Hopefully, you have discovered Him and will love Him with all of your heart. The salvation part is great and all, but the actual relationship with Jesus is the icing on the cake, it's like the gold medal. It is more rewarding than anything else on this earth. So, when people die, my first thought is, "I wonder if they knew and accepted Jesus? Will I see them in Heaven?" And I feel that way about everyone, even very close family members. Especially the ones that I am not quite sure if they know my Jesus. If they really understand that Jesus came so that they could be near God? Dwell with God when they leave Earth. My heart begs them to know that Jesus really did love them to death. To some it seems like it's really none of my business but actually it kind of is. It's the point of Jesus saying to His disciples to go and spread the Good News. That's for you and me too. If you feel like you have done nothing else in this world but openly talk about God, then I would commend you. You have done a great deal of good, a great deal of something that is meaningful, and you will hear words of affirmation from God when you see him.

Jesus said to His Father, within hours before his death on the cross, in John 17:3 "Now this is eternal life: that they know you, the only true God and Jesus Christ whom you have sent." Knowing Him is the only way. Hear me when I say it doesn't mean being incredibly religious. You are just asking God into your heart, becoming a disciple, then helping others do the same, understanding that you can turn from sin and follow Him. It says in scripture that those who believe in Jesus as the Messiah would believe in your heart and confess with your mouth. And there is no perfection expected either. Jesus was the only perfect one. As I consider the chains of religion, it was suggested to me to get baptized. Once we became members at our church I wanted to make the public profession as well. My husband at the time asked me if I had been sure I asked Jesus into my heart and life as protocol before doing so. Now, I have never been a religious person, but it was perfectly understandable. Yet it was a reminder of what I don't understand of Religion sometimes. Being that I did not have to endure all the ritual or judgmental religion, I have had no idea. It makes me more focused on the words of Jesus. Truth is we hardly stepped foot in church, like, ever, unless my mom's best friend invited us to Easter or Christmas events at her church. I have no idea why there are so many different denominations of Christianity. It's all still foreign to me all the different ways each church has its own ritual's. Maybe I should call them traditions.

But because of my ex-husband's background - and I think, in part, wanting to cover all the bases - he asked me those things. Not long after, I did get baptized, but not because it seemed like an answer or an absolute need for salvation. Instead, it was more of a proclamation. It was to share my belief with my church family. Also, Jesus asked John the Baptist to baptize Him, so maybe there is something to it. My heart wanted all the realms of heaven and earth to know that I love Jesus and wanted to follow Him. The baptism was for that purpose. He paid the huge price so that you and I could be with God, reconciled to God, His child. It's one of the reasons I wanted to write this book, to proclaim, and to glorify Him. Desperately I want others to see God's glory in my life and how I have been redeemed. There are times when it is very easy to give God His due glory. In two thousand eleven I felt God asking me to write my story down but I was disobedient for a bit. Then when I was pregnant with my youngest I finally said "yes" to God. You see, I kept telling myself that I wasn't Author material and that no one would want to read my story. In essence, I was telling God "No" and I was also telling Him that through me He could not be used. But God kept telling me to tell my story because He is there. In a mighty way for sure! Sure, my past and even my current new past is messy, but God has gotten me through it all. He will still use me. So finally after my pity party, I decided to say "Yes." Even if this could be a flop or even left unfinished. My God loves me and He would never lead me astray if I am in obedience to him. So I write. And here we are.

When I sit here I have tears because I am flabbergasted that God wants me. The poor white-trash girl from everywhere and nowhere. The girl with no real future, who dwells on the fact that there was no clear direction to go. Uh, sometimes there still isn't. Who felt uncalled and alone most of her life. All those things I definitely am, or was, and I am sinful and do not deserve an ounce of mercy or grace. But the words in the best-selling book told me something else. When you find out who you are in Christ, you not only find answers to questions; but you all of a sudden want to be worthy. You find out to **whom** you belong. You want to change. I found out that I am a daughter of the MOST HIGH KING. I am a simple, simple person, so I can only explain it in simple terms. All I know is that this peace I have comes from the Word of God. It comes from the Prince of Peace. Despite any heartache, or darkness that comes to me, my hope is found in Him and that is all I need to get through this life. Every day I do my best to give all the honor and glory to God. That may be my only purpose in life, to give my life to God and say "Well, it's not much but here ya go, do with it what ya want." It's literally all I got.

In my times of sad reflection or when a song like "I'll Be Missing You" by Sean Puffy plays, it takes me back to a sorrowful time. I miss my sister. Greatly. But that song will play at the perfect time, while I'm in the car. Thinking about her. Suddenly, she's right there sitting next to me. I can feel her smiling. That huge, toothy smile that puffs out her cheeks. Sometimes I'll look in the rearview mirror as though she's there in the backseat. I'm singing with a smile and big puddles of water in my eyes. My heart is pounding with joy but sadness too. I have to keep blinking to see the road ahead. Which reminds me of the journey of my life. Annoyed with the water I kept trying to blink the water out of my sight. Yet, I still couldn't see the road ahead. It was just a big wet blur. Then, I read a book and it changed me from the inside out. The blur on the world was gone.

April Thirtieth
Nineteen Ninety-seven

Corinthians 5:6 So we are always confident, even
though we know that as long as we live in these
bodies, we are not home with the Lord.

The door is loud. A frantic loud. I finally wake up, and she's there, scared! Repeating over and over that she can't find them. She can't find her babies. I am fully awake now. She steps into my Memaw's room, just a couple of steps away, and tells her the same thing.

I lived with my grandmother in her one-bedroom cabin on the lake. A month or so before, she had gone to Arizona to spend time with her husband, so I stayed at her cabin to watch over it. When she got back home, I kind of just kept living there. I slept in the big orange chair in the living room which was right next to Memaw's room. I still had all of my belongings at mom's house, but I jumped around and would spend the night with Memaw and a couple of my friends.

My mom was trusting and great about it. It might have bothered her, but she never really said that to me.

Mom is kind of loud with me. Rushing me with this overwhelming sense of urgency. Memaw keeps asking her questions, and Mom is frantic with no answers. The same answer "I can't find them, they are gone!" "Come help me look for them. They can't be far; their shoes are still home." We are trying to figure out what to do next as we run out the door and into my car. As we are leaving, she yells at Memaw to call the police for us. Instantly my thoughts are *Do we really need to get the police involved? Surely we'll get down there and find out they're playing a trick on Mom or something, hiding, maybe getting themselves something to eat, and Mom just missed seeing them leave.* Positive thoughts fill my mind as we jump into the blue Honda that my uncle had given me after I got my license at eighteen. Surely we will get down there and they will be waiting for us.

We drive up the hill, and around the curve, and up another hill, and down a hill till we are at mom's house. Jumping out of the car she proceeds to tell me that the backpacks and their shoes are still here, which gives her the conclusion that they are somewhere around. They couldn't already be at school. Besides, how would they have gotten there since they rode the bus? We start yelling for them. Rushing around. Yelling both of their names, but it's so quiet. Over and over we are both yelling for them. But it's very silent out in the country. It's just the crack of dawn so the light is pink tinted with dark trees stretching to the sky and you can hear the small creeks. Our house was just a short walk to the lake, which we had done so many times. Briefly I considered going there to look as well but changed my mind because I doubt they would go that far. Especially with no shoes on. We look in the house again and again. I do whatever she tells me to do and I look everywhere outside. We walked all over our yard which was a lot to do since there was a lot of terrain on half an acre or more.

We lived in a subdivision, but it's a fixer upper home on a huge lot with a small creek that runs through the land. Mom fell in love with the place after my parents' divorce. It really needed work, but it would be ours and we would be together. Didn't matter that there was no air or heat, or that there was not a stitch of carpet on those concrete floors. It would have been a great house if we'd had the money to fix it up. My favorite Uncle and Memaw helped mom get it, and we were thankful! Our little house on the side of a small hill. The house where Mom's pot belly pig ran loose but never seemed to get out of our yard. Most likely because we lived almost like in a valley so it was a tough climb for a fat pig. I can still hear it squealing when I recall a memory from there.

I'm confused, but I'm not really worried yet. *Where could they be? Why are they hiding?* Mom seems more frantic. We went up the hill to all the neighbors who we knew or at least to houses the kids played at sometimes. It's still so early. Most people are up and getting ready for school though. I still don't know what to think. Finally the Officer shows up to take the report of my siblings missing. Standing there in our steep driveway I can see my mom is really worried. It's in her eyes and in her voice. Having children of my own, I now understand.

But still, I don't believe anything life changing or tragic has happened. Family changing. The Officer is there asking us questions. Who do we think could have taken them? *What? Take them? Why would someone do that?* All the questions he asks and we answer them all honestly and those questions now have led me to more of my own questions. At one point I look at mom and remind her that I need to get to school. It's my senior year, and I've missed so much school due to Scarlet Fever and other illnesses'. Suddenly my thoughts are about the fact that I'm worried about not possibly graduating. I'm actually more afraid of missing school than not finding my sibling because surely my siblings are goofing around some place. There is no way I think or believe that something has happened to them. But I may not graduate if I miss another day.

It's April 30, 1997. Graduation is so close I can taste it. I'm the oldest and first to graduate from high school and it's important to me to finish. My mom had just gotten her GED the year before, and honestly I'm not a huge fan of school. The only subjects I like are English and Phys. Ed., and I despise the social aspect of it all. So to think that I would have to redo my senior year or have the embarrassment of having to go to summer school and not walking across the stage was gut wrenching. Besides, my brother and sister would turn up any minute, and I didn't think otherwise. Being sort of certain of this all- I left my mom there with the Officer in the driveway and I raced off to get dressed for school and rush the fifteen miles to get there on time. Doing so would be seen as something horrible later. Not only would that be viewed as an action of some sort of guilt but it would be seen as my part in helping the killer. But how did we know that my baby brother and sister were in danger? How did we know any of what had transpired in the wee hours of that morning? How did we know that what had happened would change our lives drastically? That it was life taking in so many ways. People say it all the time, and I do still, you never think anything horrible will happen to you or your family. Most certainly not someone murdering a beloved. But stuff can happen to anyone. ANYONE. I don't think anyone is protected from the evil things that can happen. *Satan is the ruler of this earth, and he's here to steal, kill and destroy.* He makes the bad in the world…not God.

The drive to school is fuzzy. Living on the outskirts of town it took twenty minutes to get there. Plenty of time to think; to replay the whole morning and night before over in my head. I'm gripping the steering wheel *tight*. White knuckle tight. The music is really loud. Just to forget for a minute. The further I got from my house the more my belly hurt. Once I parked I couldn't stop thinking about them. All of a sudden a part of me wanted to go back to my mom. My baby brother and sister. My baby siblings. *Where in the world were they? Maybe I should go back and help mom.* Half dazed, I do my best to get in the routine of school. Being that I wasn't sure what I should be feeling, there were no tears. Truth is at an early age I was tough and I felt like crying showed a bit of weakness. Like you couldn't handle things or something. My mom was someone who cries easily. The woman would cry at every sappy movie or sweet gesture. Sadly I would get annoyed at her tears because she really was so tenderhearted. My heart wasn't that tender then. But boy do I regret making fun of her because I think that there is something that happens after you have children. Sometimes you turn into this mushy mush pot. For me the water works start at songs and gestures and even just thoughts of people that are dear to me. It's ridiculous! Just the other day I cried while chatting with my second daughter. We watched a commercial on TV with a baby. All we were doing was talking about how you start out so tiny, and then you grow and grow, and then you can go on and do big things in life. I cried. Cried because of a commercial. Just like my mom. Maybe you reap what you laugh about!

After a couple of classes I was called into the Principal's Office. My teacher looked at me in amazement and I replied that I wasn't in trouble. I knew what she was thinking because I was a kid who never got into trouble. I mumbled to her it was that my brother and sister were missing. Pretty sure I heard the class gasp. Trembling all the way to that office my head thought of all the reasons they called me. Scared. I had never been in the office before; a straight-and-narrow student who had never seen the inside of any disciplinary school office. Academically and socially I was a nobody. That student no one really noticed, just an average, run-of-the-mill girl trying to get out of there with a diploma. Not the popular cheerleader, not the cool nerd, and definitely not the pretty social butterfly either. A complete nobody.

Once at the Principal's office, there was an Officer there waiting for me. A hot flash came over me with nausea. First of all, because I knew that this meant something bad. He asked me a few questions. A couple of them I had already answered in my driveway that morning with the first Officer. There was nothing new to offer and he has nothing new to share. They were still missing. *Wait, what? Still missing?* I am even more scared now. Another hot wash came over me and very often after that. A little panic attack.

That became a God to me. The God of Panic. That's when fear and panic attacks really started for me and sometimes Panic will flare her ugly head in my life now. But back then it was stealing my life. Suddenly I became a slave to fear. Paralyzed. My world was so wrapped up in fear that it showed on my thin body. How can anyone eat when you're so afraid to breathe? One time while at school a big panic attack swept over me so overwhelming that it stopped me in my tracks. It had been a week or so after her death. It was on my way walking outside to go to my next class and I guess I was thinking about her and I shouldn't have been. School was a great distraction but my mind was consumed with the events that were going on personally in my life. But I remember this day like it was yesterday. One minute I'm walking to class. Suddenly fear crashed over me and I stopped to sit down. There I was sitting on the ground, nauseous and unable to move. Paralyzed. Feeling out of control and almost afraid I would pass out. All of these students are just hustling around rushing to get to the next class. No one realized that Panic was all over me and she was fierce. I didn't realize it then but that was just the beginning. That was my life, and praise to the true God I would eventually learn how to free myself from that cruelty of panic. I read this great book and it changed me. To be honest, I've even been on and off anxiety meds when I believe I need it. Still there are plenty of things I do not do now because I do have anxiety about social situations. For instance I don't sing in the Worship band like I'd like and I get a little anxious before going out with friends sometimes. For no reason. Sure, it's something that I still deal with, but it's not my ruler anymore. Life hasn't stopped like it once did so long ago. I am not a slave to the fear. I'm fully aware of what a lie it is so I move on the best I can. But the trauma of my sister's murder changed me.

After school let out my first thought was to get home as soon as possible. When I got over the hill there was a huge Command Post set up near my mom's home on the left. People everywhere. The first thing I noticed was the huge white trailer that I would later find out helps set up the Command Post. My mom was sitting on a tailgate in one of the neighbor's driveways. She looks sad and lost a little, maybe even a little angry. She would be criticized for sitting there. There were a few people around her. The fact that she sat there would be used against her. Along with something that she allegedly said. It was stated in the paper that she said, "Well there goes my child support." That statement bared no truth. Maybe someone should have checked the child support records for themselves before thinking that that statement was even something she would consider saying. Especially since child support was behind. In other words, we never relied on the child support money for us. But again, it was printed in the paper that way and it helped make her look like someone she wasn't. Helped her look like a mother who didn't care. Which blew my mind! My sweet mother.

There I sat in my car over the hill. Not really knowing where to park or if I should park. It looked like a scene out of a movie. Camera crews and people everywhere. After talking with mom, I walked over to the main area where they were sending people out to search for my sister and brother. Asking what I could do to help and then was discouraged to do so. They didn't want family to search. It may have been less than thirty minutes and they received a call of a small boy found near a cemetery by a cowboy out exercising his horse. A desolate Cemetery. This was so surreal. Seriously, again, like a movie. For some reason, I wondered if my dad had been notified? We had talked a few days before about how things weren't really going that well. We always seemed to never have enough money. Which seemed sad and crazy because Mom had at least three jobs. Sometimes I wondered if life would be such a struggle if I would have stayed with dad. So I shared with him my concerns, and it wasn't that mom was doing anything wrong. Mom was doing her very best, and I will always believe that! Maybe I just missed him. Maybe I wanted him to do more for us. Maybe I wanted him to step up and put us first. We hardly ever saw him or spoke to him and it was heart wrenching. Especially when part of your identity is wrapped up in being a daddy's girl. But all of a sudden there was no daddy around. Partly, I felt abandoned by him a little bit once I moved in with mom in the summer of ninety-four. My parents separated on Christmas when I was fourteen, but I moved in with my mom when I turned fifteen that following summer. Once I moved in with mom I think we saw dad at Christmas only. That's not saying he was a bad father, but only seeing your dad once or twice a year was an adjustment. Christmas was our time to really see dad. So, I missed him.

My dad would be there soon. To our little town on the lake. In a way, I couldn't wait to see him. Just see his face, and my grandmother who was his mother. They both were my rock people, I mean, the people that you just stand next to and you feel better. You just know that everything is going to be ok. Later, I met them at their hotel. All of my dad's side of the family seemed to be in the town we lived in. My uncles, aunts, and cousins. There were a lot of my dad's side of the family and we used to do everything together. But after the divorce, it wasn't the same so the fact that nearly everyone was there surprising. The gang was all back together.

The call they had gotten about a boy found in a cemetery turned out to be my baby brother. We followed the Authorities over to the next Command Post which was the area that they found my youngest brother at. The road to get to the cemetery he was found in is so old and complicated to get to if you don't know where to go. It's near a creek and a bunch of land. He was taken to the hospital immediately. A cowboy had found him inside the cemetery while he was out riding his horse. He heard him crying out. I can't imagine how scary that might have been. His head had been beaten severely. He had been there for hours in the sun, dried plasma at the back of his head, eaten up by ants and alone. He told the paramedic's and whoever else was around that the bad man had done this to him. He named him by name. I'll be honest, if I start to think about the fact that he must have been frantic about where she was; I sink. My stomach turned a little. This little nine-year-old boy who had apparently tried to protect his big sister would soon find out that she was gone. That all his efforts were fruitless. Unfortunately, there is a real chance he felt as though her death was his fault. The weight of that I have felt as well, but I was not there with her in that car. I'm telling you I can't go there mentally. I can't sit here and imagine them in that dumb car driving, so scared; so battered already. To think about the chaos and the fear they must have experienced. It makes me angry and filled with deep sadness. Truthfully, I don't go there in my mind for so many reasons. The main one is that my sister is with Jesus and she doesn't think about that. But my baby brother on the other hand, it's a burden, oh and painfully a memory that I would do almost anything to take that away from him.

Thankfully, I never saw him there inside the cemetery, because by the time I drove there he was moved to the hospital. There then was a new Command Post near the cemetery. Of course I was discouraged again to go search with them. So, I sat there. Looking around at all the people who were scouring and searching as far as the eye could see. I felt helpless and afraid. There I sat thinking that I would see this beautiful white-haired beauty walk up safe and sound. I mean, what else would be the outcome? Finally, I left that Command Post at the cemetery after a few minutes longer and headed to the hospital to see my brother. I would visit that cemetery nineteen years later. It has these beautiful trees that arch over the road near the area where the cowboy found him. You would never think that a little boy was left there to die almost two decades before.

His wounds were too old to do much of anything but stitch up. He had strangled marks around his neck and ant bites all over his body. His head had been beaten against a headstone a few times, but the injuries were not life threatening. He went to the Children's Hospital to be watched over to be sure his injuries wouldn't get worse. Thank goodness he lived. He is alive and well today. But there was a different story in regard to his injuries that was told. The newspapers and Prosecutors said he had suffered such a blow to the head that he had parts of his skull break off into his brain. But that wasn't true. I didn't realize how the media would just get information wrong. It's one reason that I never trust what the Media says anymore. I know from my own experience with newspapers and journalists that they don't seem to get all the facts before publishing. Or they report one sided. That can definitely ruin someone's life. Media isn't all bad but I don't trust them. I never watch the news. I get what's happening in the world through the little bit of social media I'm on. Even still I have trust issues with the media.

My youngest brother is well into adulthood now. My father and stepmom received custody of him after all of this happened so I can't account for much of his life then or even after. I stayed in the area to be near mom and memaw for a little while. So I can't write about all that he went through afterwards. One time I was asleep on the living room floor at my dad's house and all of a sudden my dad came running down that hallway to my brother's room. My brother was having a nightmare and dad had developed an ear for listening to them at night. After the terror and excitement of the episode I cried thinking about what he must have seen in his nightmare. Lingering damage that had been done. Most likely to subside with age but not leave till eternity. He dealt with other issues as well, but those are his stories to tell. With victory or with current overcoming. I've always felt like God would use him in his lifetime. He's not done with my brother yet. Might be a lot of pressure too, unless you know that you know that you are a child of God and he only has plans to prosper you. I know he believes in Jesus. So the rest is his business.

Early Beginnings

You take our failure, you take our weakness. You set your treasure in jars of clay. ... The world sees your life in me.
– Broken Vessels, Hillsong

Growing up our family was pretty normal to me. Happy. Close knit family who never did much without each other. I mean all seventeen of us spread out anywhere we went. We would go out to eat at Golden Corral and it seemed like controlled chaos. During the Holidays we spent them wherever Grandma and Grandpa were. It was my Grandparents, my dad's oldest brother, his wife and their two boys. My other uncle and his wife and her three children, and then my dad, mom, and us four kids. Most of the time we would live within walking distance to each other, even a few times we all lived in the same subdivision. However, we did move a lot, which apparently had something to do with my father not being able to pay rent. Which itself is crazy, but then you add in the fact that his whole family pretty much moved when we would and that seems unheard of. We were tight knitted and it was rewarding for many reasons. Grandma, my father's mom, was our rock. She was the glue that kept the family together. That woman was the epitome of the perfect grandma. She baked big, beautiful cakes, hunted deer and squirrels, fished, cooked from scratch, could sew anything, spanked your bottom when needed, and laughed with you. A real classic beauty too, in fact apparently her fifth cousin or something like that was a famous actress. She told me a story once of her and taking a convertible and cruising. I wish I would have asked more questions then and found out more about my family history. But we take for granted the adults in our life when we are young.

Since I am the first granddaughter, our bond felt special. In fact I may have been more of a grandma's girl than a daddy one. She was my all-time favorite person. Her words were careful, truthful but always with love. Once she took me fishing and I asked to try smoking. She was a smoker and I wanted to try it, so after a little bit, she made me light one myself and then smoke it. All confident and happy standing on a big rock I was fishing from. I took one puff of that cigarette and nearly fell into the water. My goodness she laughed so hard while I thought I was going to die right there. Times like that she did life with me honestly. In a very honest way. I never became a smoker by the way. I think that one experience was all I needed. We would have life lesson talks that I think helped shape me into who I am. She treated me as though I was something better or smarter and not like the child I was. That's part of the reason I talk with my children like I do. She gave me that example. There is no time like the present to share with them the big stuff too. Jesus or why the sky is blue; it is all relevant and it starts a bond that will surely last a lifetime.

Most of my childhood my grandma and grandpa lived with us. Recalling all of the places we lived is really fun actually. We have lived in a few states. Mostly though, we have lived in one State but all over one of its biggest metroplexes. Little towns all over. So many places. Sitting around reminiscing about the different homes with different things that happened there. Like one time we lived close to my dad and his brother's mechanic shop and went there a lot. Sometimes we would go to work with my dad and sit mostly in the greasy smelly office up at the shop. Once though, dad left my brother there and didn't realize it until after we made it home and Mom asked where he was and dad raced back to grab him. He was cool, just hanging out like nothing happened. I remember that there was a blackberry shrub that we could go pick from when at the shop as well. Just eat them right off the bush. They were a highlight of our lives then, in fact, mom would pick them and sell them for extra money. Next to the berries we would pick were huge fragrant honeysuckle vines. Of course we would gobble up the honeysuckle as well. I planted honeysuckle in my own backyard because it smells so good but it also reminds me of my grandma. I haven't been able to pull the sweet yellow part from the flower yet; but I know it's coming and it'll take me back.

My mom tells me that I went to kindergarten around this time and didn't like my teacher very much so I would spell my words, everything I did during school backwards, perfectly. Mrs. Kindergarten teacher was not fond of me being left-handed, so she tried to get me to be right-handed, and because of that … I pretended to be dyslexic. But as soon as mom reminded me that I would have to repeat Kindergarten I was healed of my dyslexia! There was no way I wanted to go back to Kinder. A few years later, in second grade, I remember a place we moved to and for some reason I can picture it decorated for Halloween. The building looks the same only it appears they have added onto it. There are also ironic places too, like the fact that we lived in a townhome when my sister was born which is sort of adjacent to where she is buried. There is a burger joint on the end of the street and we would feel rich when we could afford to eat there. Down the street is the Elementary School we attended for a very short period of time. That playground was gravel instead of rubber tires so when you fell off the equipment you would usually bleed. There's another town we lived in and I fell in love with the Drill Team and Dance. Then we lived in a place where the neighbor had a horse and he taught me to ride. There were hills so it was exhilarating while riding. I felt like I would fall off sometimes. Then another place we moved to where we were next to railroad tracks and the house was all rock. It had a chicken coop and a mother-in law unit. But we never stayed in one place long. Hop, hop, hop, that's really what we did. Honestly there is no way I can remember them all.

Some stick out because of what happened while living there. Like the trailer park we lived in with my Grandparents and my dad's baby brother's family lived down the street. In that trailer park my friend's dad touched me inappropriately after he sent my friend to bed. He told me while we sat watching wrestling that sometimes you tickle people there. My face felt so flush, my stomach turned flips and I jumped up and told him I felt sick so I wanted to go home. Thankfully, he let me call my mom to let her know that I felt sick. My friend was sound asleep as I grabbed my stuff and flew home as fast as I possibly could. Never saying a word to anyone about what happened that night. I stuffed that down to never repeat until in my thirties. One big metroplex area we lived in wasn't much different as far as moving around, we still hopped around the different cities. But it did become different for my grandmother and her other two sons. After a couple places they all moved to one trailer park, but this time they each bought instead of renting. We however did not. While they all lived in the same park we lived a good twenty minutes away. This big city never felt like home to me. It was the first time we were more split up. The weather seemed oppressive, the drivers impatient and I missed the country. My family still hopped around skipping rent sometimes but the rest of the family settled down. It felt weird and different. We weren't hopping together anymore.

My parents were married young, but not because they were pregnant with me like I thought for many years. My mom was sixteen and my dad was eighteen. They fell in love when my mom was fourteen and decided that they would spend forever together. I found an awesome marriage newspaper clipping and it was surreal to see this whole print out of this young couple. My parents, and their dreams were written down for the whole town to see. Weird too because I didn't realize that it was such a big thing to do for my parents. For so long I thought that I was the reason for the young marriage. Mom got pregnant with me after they were married, so she was seventeen when she gave birth to me. I can't even imagine. At that age, my biggest concern was what my Arby's work schedule was. Mom had dropped out of school after eleventh grade, and Daddy was doing technical school to be a mechanic. Daddy turned out to be a fantastic mechanic. That man can fix anything, well, if you ask me. Like one time I drowned my Honda during a flash flooding storm and he pulled me out and put that car back together for me. That car drove for a couple more years after that. Seriously, my Daddy can fix anything.

So after they had me in January of nineteen ninety-seven, they had my brother in December of the same year. Irish twins. I'll never know how she did it. Or if she felt like she did it, but to have two kids only ten months apart is madness! They suffered the loss of a baby boy to SIDS a couple of years after my Irish twin was born. Vaguely I remember paramedics there. Someone was over the cradle he was in. My brother and I thought we did something wrong. It was in the middle of the night. The baby had already passed away, sound asleep. We sat there thinking about the day, doing our best to recall if there was something that we did to hurt him. Pictures of the baby in his tiny casket are the only thing I remember from the funeral. He was dressed in blue and white. It was eerie to look at since it was this little infant in a casket, who looked like a doll lying there. It seems so unfair to lose something when it was still so fresh to the world. Doesn't really make it easier either, or I know that it was hard for them. The other day I saw a picture of them that was taken the day of the funeral for him. This old picture of these two young people that seemed so sad. They were standing up both dressed in black clinging to each other and you could see the sorrow in their eyes. They would suffer another great loss many years later, but only not clinging to each other this time. It's unfortunate and hard to imagine that they both lost two children so young. They themselves were so young and have endured great sadness that many have not.

My parents had my sister about seven years after the baby's death. Daddy came home to tell us that we had a baby sister and she had lots of white hair. He said she looked like an angel with a halo. Apparently she had white hair that kind of went around her forehead and it reminded him of a halo. Everyone always said she was the most beautiful baby. Not your old man looking kind of baby, she was absolutely heavenly looking. Right away I told everyone I had a twin! The excitement of having a sister was overwhelming! I'm not sure why since I was about seven when she was born but I thought we were twins. Ha! Her arrival was a joyous time for sure.

After her came my youngest brother about four years later. Feisty from the beginning. Little bitty thing too. He was like our little dress up doll at this point because I was eleven years old. My girl cousins and I would dress him up like our baby daughter and we even called him "Codeine." He was pretty non combative about it. I'm pretty sure he loved it too! After having my youngest brother my parents decided to remedy the baby making and my mom had her tubes tied. A family of six now with less than middle class wage. But we were a happy family outside of the fact that we were financially struggling. I remember Mom telling me about one time Dad took a loaf of bread, bologna, and cheese from the store because we didn't have much to eat. She was seven months pregnant and apparently Dad went back later to pay the store manager but he wouldn't let him. I've never asked him about it either and probably never will. I'm sure it's not his proudest moment. You can tell by the fact that he went back to pay for it that he had integrity and values. That he felt convicted about his wrongdoing but also I wonder if he felt trapped? Sometimes you get caught up in a position of taking care of your family that you make a decision that wasn't right. My Dad was what you would call a dreamer. He still is and I love him for that. I always have. He and his brothers have been on business ventures together attempting to make life better. I'm thankful for that spirit of being ambitious with progressive thinking. We tell our children to dream big and go do what is on your heart to do. I wanted more in life too. Not it all, but just more. So my dad being a dreamer made me feel like it was ok to dream as well. He wasn't afraid.

One of my uncles on my dad's side was in a band with my Dad. He was a drummer and he taught me one summer when I was thirteen how to play, and I thought I wasn't too shabby. I bought a drum set after that- never thought about going on the road or anything but it was like a birthright or something. Since Dad and Uncle played music together, they played quite a bit in old Honky Tonks. We tagged along as much as we could, especially when we were younger. Even up until after high school they played in a Country Western band together and the family would go and support them. Those are some of my favorite memories. It's where my deep love for music started. Where my dream of becoming the next famous singer came from.

This Uncle passed away not long after my sister and then his mom, my grandma, died not long after that. My favorite Grandma.

There was no way I could go to her funeral. Oh, my heart. It felt like tragedy came to my doorstep all over again. Basically I wanted to die. Life wouldn't stop handing me out loss. Losing another person I loved and cherished. In less than three years I lost three of the most important people in my life, on top of all the stuff that was going on with my mom and her trial and prison. Normal life was gone. Gone. Grandma's death was almost as devastating to me as my sister's. Since we lived hours apart, I hadn't seen her in a while. At the time all my extra money was used to drive to see my mom, who was in Prison almost three hours away. So other visits were put on the back burner, which wasn't one of my finer season's. There seemed to only be so much I could juggle, considering that I was in relationship after relationship that I needed to put effort in those as well. Convicted with guilt and anger at myself when I received the call that she passed, my life felt even more dark. Just like that, she was gone; there would be no more porch talks. I would never hug her fragile body again or hear her tiny voice on the phone. I coveted the way she would say my name. Still now I hear it faintly when trying to recall it. It was home to my soul. But this was during my really hard anxiety riddled time in life so I could not bring myself to go to her funeral. There was no way I could have looked at her little body there in that coffin without collapsing with sadness. No way I would have made it to the funeral without being so physically ill that it would be nearly impossible to drive. So I chose to be a coward that day. Honestly, writing this I am blubbering like a baby. But before she passed she would write to me though and I would write to her. In my home those cards and letters are around to keep her alive here in my space. In my home. One of my prize possessions was a postcard she sent from a trip she took with a gentleman she met. She looked happy and carefree. There was always so much to glean from her, and I am told that I am so much like her. I hope I am half the person she was. I miss her, and I hope that if she is looking down on my life that she is pleased. I can't wait to run into her arms. Hear her same my name. Heaven can't get here soon enough.

So, while my dad and his brothers were trying to make it in the world, my mom was a stay-at-home mom with an eleventh grade education. She was a hard worker when she needed to be but I think having four kids before the age of 25 was a lot. Surely it was hard and lonely at times. I had four kids by the time I was 34! She may not have had big dreams but I do know that she wanted to work with children or horses. She loved horses and grew up around them for a period. Her love of horses rubbed off on me, and my second daughter. There really is no telling what a young version of my mom would have done with her life after we were all in school. A different path chose her instead, so she was left with no real choice. One thing that I think about at times is pondering if Mom was depressed. In fact, she was so bad at keeping a clean home. I bring this up because it was a big deal to the media people too. To the District Attorney. They painted her as a bad mother because her house was dirty and someone said she said something awful. But she will be the first to agree with you on the fact that she's not great at keeping a clean house. Only two of my good friends ever got invites to my house, for fear of judgment. This may be where my obsession with a clean house stem from. I'll admit this too, that while I have a clean house, I have let it steal my joy many times. Cleaning in circles when I should just be enjoying my kids and being present. So, I get it. Who needs a clean house when you have four mini tornadoes! That doesn't mean I am a better Mom than she is or was. By no means, in fact I think at times that she was a more patient mom, nope, she really was a more patient mom than I can be. I am too much of a perfectionist, and obsessed with making sure things are orderly and most of the time I forget about giving out grace to my own little people.

To me, it didn't make her a horrible mother, just an untidy one. Devoted to us she would listen to our words. Even with all of her odds and end jobs she did her best to get me the things I needed and sometimes desired. Oh, and she always, always believed in us. Constantly telling us we could do or be whatever we wanted to be in life. Anything. Honestly, that is so much more to a child than a spotless house and brand name clothes. So much more to a child than being lavished with expensive toys or big blowout bash birthday parties. Those things are so temporary. But when you have a Momma like we had, you aren't tied down to your circumstances or to what the world thinks of you! Even to what you think of yourself. You really do ponder if you could fly! Being a mom myself now I understand how judgmental others can be. Thank goodness my mom didn't have Pinterest to beat her down too. Today so many moms are trying to do it all. Fit this incredibly unattainable mold of perfection. A lot of times I am told that I'm supermom. Raising four kids nearly singly and still being kind and a servant is apparently incredible. Truth is, I'm just doing my life like someone who is grateful and in love with God. I have learned that there is a season for everything. There is no way to do everything for your kids and for yourself that you would love to do. There will be choices you have to make. No matter how bad you want too, you must think about what is at stake. If it's a calling or what you are passionate about it then it will be there when you can say "yes". If it's just being on the PTO at your child's school or serving in a capacity at church that you can't. Don't worry because it will be there when the timing is better and you will be glad you didn't overload yourself. There is a season for everything. And even if your heart aches to serve in a capacity that doesn't make rest available, then just wait. The moms who think they have it all are the ones who feel like they have reached a harmonious life. They understand that children are such a worthy and valuable ministry and they need present parents. I call it one of my greatest ministries to serve in ever. We won't be needed by them in the same way forever. It will change, but we are responsible for the little people that God is loaning to us. We are to help work on and minister to their hearts. Precious little people that need to know one very significant thing; that he or she is the child of the Most High King! Something I've learned a lot the way is that you have to give out loads of grace to your little people as well. I may miss doing that myself sometimes. Maybe my parents didn't really instill in us more than the fact that we were Christians and believed in God. But I was always sure of them loving me. As a family we didn't get to experience Disney World or trips to Colorado or even eating out at the best restaurants. Our clothing stores were Goodwill and Thrift shops and we ate our stock in bologna sandwiches. But let me tell you this, I never felt unloved.

The family always did the best they could for each other. I never knew that we were really that poor or considered the fact that not every family was big like ours. I miss it because it was all I knew for fifteen years. Thankfully my kids will know family like that as well. Their Dad's family is a lot like that. They spend good amounts of time together. I know how awesome it was to grow up with all the family and cousins galore. I'm so thankful God gave my children that because so many memories will carry them through life. When they grow up those memories with cousins will be cherished ones; ones that will bring back the feeling of home. Even if they all grow apart it is still woven into their lives which is deep in all of their hearts already. It will spur them on during much needed times of their lives.

Did That Happen?

I'll be missing you. Every step I take. Every move I make.
Every single day, every time I pray, I'll be missing you.
– Sean "Puffy" Combs

Once I got to the hospital, I was scared to see my baby brother but knew that I had to. I could barely look at him though. In Fact, all I can recall is his skinny body lying there. Still a little dirty. But I can't remember his face. Only bandages but I did search for his eyes. He was terrified. I was terrified. My Mom was there holding his hand, crying. Standing there the room was spinning for me. My heart was racing with adrenaline, suddenly I was in that place, that place where you are scared that you are about to lose someone. All of a sudden fear that I may have already lost her. Seeing him like that was my first inclination that my sister may be gone. But even still, we never uttered those words. Who would think that all of this would happen? That you could lose your younger sister? A precious and vital young girl. I mean, things like that don't happen to our family! *Oh my goodness, where is she?* There was an urgency to go look for her that overwhelmed me.

He had ant bites, three open wounds on the back of his head that were old, sunburned and choke marks around his neck. The wounds on the back of his neck were from banging his head against a tombstone in the cemetery. The bruises around his neck from the bad man choking him was an inclination that he really tried to kill him. It's truly amazing that he didn't suffer more damage than what he did. He was transferred up to the Hospital for kids for a few days to keep an eye on him to make sure that his injuries were not life threatening. My mom stayed with him. She rarely left his side after that, until she was put in jail.

No doubt I had been holding it all together pretty well up until that point. At least on the outside. I really never believed that what transpired would have. But after seeing baby brother like that, beaten, and left for death, I was afraid. A sense of urgency swept over me as well too. We needed to find my sister soon. I refused to let people tell me not to help look after that. My Dad and some of the families were in town now. My heart felt better with more family in town. They had a hotel room and I went there after the hospital. My Grandmother and I sat outside while she smoked a cigarette and we talked. In her calm way she sat there and asked me all of these questions, much like interrogating, only with a calm manner. Calmly I answered them all the best I could. I knew that she was trying to take account of everything that transpired up to the day of my sibling's abduction. In my heart I wondered if she felt as scared as I did, or if she was afraid we would never see my sister again. She gave no inclination of either. But that was my grandma for you.

Before leaving, my next stop was to my dad's room to check on his plans. When I came into the room my old boyfriend was standing there with his brother. It startled me to see my first love in the same room as my dad. My dad hadn't met any friends or boyfriends since we moved after the divorce. But here he was with my first love. That one that you had to let go of but you wish you hadn't because well, it's your first love. He came by to check on me and see if he could do anything to help. I can still see him standing there in his Wranglers with his arms folded in front of him. His brother who had come with him; he would lose his life in a car accident a few years later. He was one of the nicest guys you'd ever meet. I was deeply saddened that his family had to go through that pain. I knew that pain. But I was kind of short with my first love and his brother that day. I had felt hurt by our breakup. My heart still stung with rejection. That was the last time I saw him. I wish I had been nicer or at least extended more grace. But I didn't and the brothers were gone and I would never see them again or thank them for trying to do something to help us that day. This was a hard lesson for me to learn. To extend kindness to those who reach out to you. To not be ruled by your momentary emotion.

After staying long enough to get filled in and fill everyone in I left the Hotel. Some of the family was going to the Hospital but I stayed in town. Mom said that a psychic had contacted her to let her know that she felt like my sister would be found near a bridge, by the lake and there would be a Marina sign across the way. A few acquaintances went to search over bridges for my sister so I jumped at the chance. Still I had hope that we would find her someplace and she would be safe. Honestly, I don't know that I really thought that she would be gone. All my hope was in her being someplace just left there like my brother had been. The first bridge we started on was the first one that goes into downtown. It was next to a set of train tracks that went over the lake that was always vandalized and spray painted on. Eerily we gathered together after pulling over to the side of the road before walking over the bridge. My stomach turned over and over. *Did I really want to find her? What if she was lifeless? What if she needed medical attention?* Darkness started to cover the sky, my heart in my throat, calling her name over and over. Each time I heard her name called; tears welled up. Everyone that was with me echoed her name, over and over. The guy leading it was a guy a few years older, and just like the cowboy who found my brother, I knew who he was. He still lives in town, and he wasn't much older than me, but we don't have any contact with each other. But I would tell him that he was brave to lead that search, even if we left after that because of the darkness. It made me feel less helpless for a bit of time. Maybe I was scared but also ready to stop feeling so helpless. She didn't turn up that night. Thank goodness we didn't find her ourselves that night. Her body was found the next day. By the lake, just over a bridge, near a marina with a sign. Her throat slit. Her body all cut up with a knife. Just like the Psychic that contacted my mother had said. It's eerie to think that the Psychic was pretty accurate. And now that I'm a Jesus follower, I am not sure how I feel about psychics. One thing is for sure, I'm thankful that we didn't stumble upon her that night. My scars may be a little bigger if I had. The trauma. To sit and contemplate all the bad things that surround her death. Like, I shouldn't go there. No one should. Imagine her there terrified. I think about her sadness and her heart. It must have broken into a thousand pieces. No one was there to protect her. This evil was surrounding her little body and she could go nowhere. Ugh. My heart.

Thankfully, I also know that Jesus was there with her. That he was just waiting for her. He knew what she was about to endure and he was there for her. I imagine him standing there by her. The evil she just encountered would be met with Jesus' face and that must have set all that horror in its place. Gone from her heart. And that is why I don't camp out there thinking about what she felt or saw while being killed. It's highly doubtful that I would have this understanding if I didn't now cling to God. I cling to him. Continually I want to be changed by the truth and the Word. She will be with Jesus. She won.

My other brother, who was seventeen at the time was in jail while all this was happening. Can you imagine being locked up in jail while your little sister and brother are missing? I wonder if he got updates on what was going on. He had been hanging out with a less than stellar crowd. They stole something and he got caught and put in jail. Most of them were good kids but sometimes you drink a little too much or smoke weed and something like theft sounds like fun to you! My brother has always been a great kid even now he's such a likable guy. We are woven from the same cloth he and I in that sense. But even great kids do dumb stuff just because of peer pressure. Or I don't know- our brains are not developed or something, right? They called us into a room at the police station and they brought him in there as well. Seeing him there made me even more sad. Once all the immediate family was there, they told us that she had been found. Her throat slit, and her little body stabbed repeatedly. They said that he took them to her finally. We weren't ready for that news. There was screaming and wailing in that small room. I'm not a dramatic person, but all the air left my body and I fell to my knees on the floor sobbing. When I gathered myself, I stood up and found my Irish twin and hugged him so tight. So tight, like an angry tight. We were all angry and sad at the same time. He and I were like our everything to each other which made this such a blow. We always made it our responsibility to take care of our siblings and each other so this was more than failure. I don't recall exactly what happened directly afterwards for everyone else but I had to leave. After they gave us the news about her, they released my seventeen-year-old brother to my father. I was relieved that he was able to come home. There was no reason for him to stay in jail, it was his first time to do something like that and his circumstance was devastating. He's never been back to jail. My Irish twin is one of the good ones.

After the news of my sister, I wanted to run away. I went to this park-like place with a picnic table. I cannot remember where exactly it was but I feel like it was near the lake. Pretty remote where I knew no one would see me or at least be there that time of day. I sat there and I wept. I only felt comfortable to weep alone. I chose to be outside because I felt closer to this ominous God I knew so little about. Still today, being outside makes me feel closer to God. My heart hurt so badly though and I surely wanted to tell this God all about it. For so long, looking up to the sky made my sorrow lessen. Sometimes there was hope up there. For as long as I can remember I would look up to heaven and feel something inside my spirit. Almost like someone cared, maybe even saw me. My head was spinning with sadness so all I could do was weep. Big bouts of uncontrolled pain would leave my body but it all still felt so heavy. The big tree's leaves were noisy when the breeze blew, almost in answer to my weeping. The breeze would sweep over me and my face would feel wet cold and my long hair blew wildly. Looking up I began to tell God that he didn't need another Angel. So much anger in my heart. But I felt like I was talking to a friend or something. Through each sob I said *"You didn't need her did you? I am so mad at you for taking her. Why her? Why not me even?"* It was hard to fathom that this world would not know my beautiful sister. To me the world would be a much better place with her in it than myself. So many reasons why she would be a world changer compared to me. Listening to birds and the wind blowing the leaves around; my heart was racing and I trembled, but no response from God. I wept longer there under the tree at the picnic table. All alone. All of the sorrow that overwhelmed me then I left on the picnic table. I wanted to be sure God saw me weep, that He saw my pain. Almost like there was nothing to help cover up the pain. So many questions filled my mind though. *Why? How can you go from this place of being nothing and having nothing happening to this all out tragedy?* My life was different and I was different in just a matter of two days. Once

I stood up though, I felt lighter. My heart still hurt so badly but my head was a little clearer. There was a sense of resolution that at least I had let God know how I felt. For sure I know that there is no way I knew that what I was doing was actually good for my soul. Good for revealing the wound to someone who already knew it was there. That my heavenly Father knew.

I never contemplated that maybe God understood my depth of despair. That He had walked there, watched there, even held His breath in the same way I had when His son Jesus was being hung on the cross for me. For my sister. Well, for you. There at that picnic table it was me wrestling with God. Looking back I feel like it was a little like Jacob wrestling with the "man" in the Bible. I felt like I had verbally wrestled with God from this place of complete agony. I used only words and tears but there was wrestling involved and some healing that came with that. It felt a whole lot like a fight. Maybe it felt like there was nowhere to go but up with this pain. My sweet sister was gone. A perfect little angel. Like life was gone. I wanted to sit there and maybe time would stop as well. I didn't want to face the reality of what this all meant to me now. Truth is you can't begin to put into words that even explain the depth of the pain. But my healing started there at that table. I wasn't bottled up once I gave it to God. I might have still been in pain and felt alone, but I handed over my grievances to Him. The very best I knew how, I mean, He already knows what's in your heart so that is really no hiding it from Him. He can release a lot of things for you if you allow Him. If you ask Him. I bet even if you feel unworthy too, or ashamed to be angry at Him. I bet He can handle it. He does say in Matthew 11:28, "Come to Me, all who are weary and heavy-laden, and I will give you rest."

To Depart

Corinthians 4:18 So we don't look at the troubles we can see right now; rather we look forward to what we have not see yet. For the troubles we see will soon be over, but the joys to come will last forever.

For a little more background, let's go back, but let's just go back to nineteen ninety-three. It was Christmas Eve and apparently my parents were splitting up. Yet my mom didn't know that until that day. This would be our last Christmas together as a family. My mom had no idea that she would be getting her eviction notice from Dad on Christmas Eve. My Mom had just returned from taking care of her mother after a surgery concerning cancer. Which did not make sense to my mom why Dad was so eager for her to go. She had been gone a couple of weeks and we had been looked after by a live-in Nanny -like person. We knew her from the bowling alley my parents both worked at and she was about 18. She smoked, she cursed, she had this free hippy thing about her. It was slightly weird to have her live with us and watch us since my parents were still not making great strides financially, but that whole picture would soon make more sense.

Mom got home on Christmas Eve from her trip caring for Memaw after her surgery. There was a somber mood in the air after my parents broke the news of them splitting up. Which took my brother and I by surprise. We would go ahead and open our Christmas gifts with them that night. So our joyous gift opening felt like something else. Our gifts mostly came from the Angel Tree program, but my parents would fill under the tree with as much as they could. I will always remember that Christmas for more than one reason. Being an Angel Tree recipient really helped my parents out. That year someone purchased me this super soft preppy plaid skirt with a white silk blouse along with something else I can't recall. That outfit became one of the best things a teenager who never felt good enough could have ever received. It made me feel like a million bucks! Something about wearing it made me hold my head higher. If I could hug the person who gave me my gift that year I would. Maybe it sounds weird, but when your clothes are mostly bought from thrift stores, it starts to dictate your self-worth. That outfit made a difference in my life.

Mom and the youngest loaded up in her white station wagon for her mom's. These two little kids in the middle of the night in car seats in the car. Sadly I watched her load up all that she could and then they were gone. Headed to live with my Memaw. How can you be sure that your parents don't belong together and yet be sad about it as well? That's what I felt. My mom left that cold evening with the youngest two siblings. Heading off to a new life. My Irish twin and I stayed there with Dad. It was my freshman year and I wanted to finish it out where I was and I didn't want to leave Dad. Also, I had a boyfriend and when you are a teen, your life is super important. You think your social life is more important than anything! There was no anger at Dad; I was just stunned and a tiny bit confused. Misguided too, since

I thought that this would give us a chance to bond. Apparently I was blind as bat as well because I didn't think about the fact that Dad and our Nanny were now in this free new relationship. Being teenagers we were a little naive. It's not like we hated who would soon be our stepmom, but we didn't understand what was going on. She was only four years older than me so it was kind of weird to listen to her like she was another Mommy or something. My Dad and she did get married when she was nineteen. And we came to love her and respect her later. They were cute together, and yet very different. I did enjoy visiting them after my sister's death. She was very welcoming and I know she loved us, and that she still does. They only stayed together married for maybe ten years. They split up but have never officially divorced. I'll be honest, I hated that. I would prefer them together, but if there is no happiness or love, then it isn't working. Yet, my desire to have my stepmom there to help my dad was selfish. He and my brothers still do things with her and her family for holidays, and vacations, and of course she helped raise my youngest brother; so they are more like family to him especially.

My parents have been divorced since I was fifteen; I mean it didn't take too long for that to happen. There wasn't a fight over custody of us kids and the assets were few. In the summer of ninety-four I still lived with my dad. At this point all of my siblings were five hours away, which made me a little lonely. Since finishing my freshman year, I considered sticking it out with Dad and his girlfriend, but I was also starting to hang out with people that I shouldn't in our trailer park. Guys older than me for starters. Thank goodness I was too scared to let them talk me into making bad choices. When summer was about to end I asked to go visit Mom, so Daddy let me. He put me on a plane and my intentions were to come back. But I couldn't. Sometimes I remember that plane ride vividly. Looking out the plane window at the clouds; it was already in the back of my mind that I might not come back to Dad. At first my thoughts were purely that I would visit mom and the kids and then come back home to Dad. But I couldn't leave my mom and siblings once I got there. My brother was there too and he had already planned on staying there with mom. My mom never really pushed the agenda that I should just stay with her and the kids. But I had always felt like the protector of those young siblings. Sounds silly I know. But being the oldest girl, I felt like I did everything that was needed when no one else was around to do so. From an early age I felt responsible for them, maybe felt like another mother to them. At a young age I could do chores and fetch things for mom. Partly since I think mom suffered from depression but also because Grandma taught me small things that I could do. By the age of eight my skills in vacuuming and making sweet tea were pretty good. Sometimes the oldest get a bad rap for being bossy and such but let's be honest by the time the second or third kid comes along, they have little people to boss around. There is this desire to take care of others when you're the oldest girl. And sometimes Mom's ask for a ~~little~~ help from the oldest.

Finally the question came up about when I was going back to home to Dad. There was this elephant in the room and she knew that she relied on me a little bit more than I wanted. She asked for me to help a lot. Course I have an oldest daughter and I wonder if I ask too much of her. Who knows? But I stayed with my little people. Stayed there with mom and I didn't go back home to Dad. Not sure how Dad felt about it. He never really said and I can't remember if he even put up a fight. In fact he didn't even tell us when he got married. Not one word. Not one invite, not a whisper until after the fact. His own children! A big part of me thinks that he didn't have the courage to tell us. He didn't need approval, I know. Who cares about whether it would have mattered to us, or the fact that he's an adult and can do what he wants. Why not a quick phone call to your four children to let them know they are about to officially have a stepmom. This nonchalant attitude was hurtful. It felt a lot like a slap in the face, and a smidge like being tossed aside. Ok, a lot tossed aside.

We first moved to a different city than my Memaw for the summer of ninety-four in an apartment and then my mom found a house near Memaw before school started. We were staying with mom's boyfriend in his apartment and since she was starting out he let us stay till summer wound down. Also, the relationship was winding down, so there were no permanent plans to stay there with him. Instead, mom looked for a house so that we could be near Memaw. The house was in my Memaw's neighborhood, so it was perfect. The house needed cleaning up a bit before we moved in and it was a little bit of a fixer upper. Before we knew it, fall was here and school started and life began new. It was different. Not only did we have new surroundings but the family looked a little different as well. There were no longer my dad's clan or cousins around. It was my mom's oldest brother and my Memaw that would be our new tribe. It was a big adjustment. Our family was my mom's mom, Mom's brother, and his wife and her daughter. It looked so different for us. Life looked different now. My Uncle and Memaw did so much for us too. I could never thank them enough. From clothes to start school with to even food on the table when we first made the move. We made lots of new friends in the neighborhood which was nice for transitioning. A couple of those good friends I've kept in contact with. We made new memories there as well. Our tragedy will never erase all the good or all the overcoming that I think mom did on her own little by little. Which is important since it's not an easy task to be forced out on your own with two little kids in tow. It's not easy starting from scratch with four kids on your own … but it's possible.

Mom had to find work and then started to get her GED so that she could get into technical school to find a vocation. She did so fantastic in school. It's sad but I was surprised how smart my mom really was. Graduated in the top of her class which to me is a big deal, because I never went to any schooling after I graduated. Never had the nerve or true desire, so I will always be so proud of her. Going to school I think proved that she wasn't just some dumb lady with an eleventh-grade education. High School was hard for me so I felt so proud of her for sticking with it and making it look effortless. The woman has brains and perseverance. But this is also a sad part too. Because of what would happen to her later, she was never actually able to use this education for more than a few months. Something that she worked hard at accomplishing and would be great at, she can't even live out now. Instead she has to settle for any job that she can get. Breaks your heart when you know how hard it is to decide- hey, I'm going to get my diploma, keep two jobs, take care of four kids, and then start technical school so that my children's lives are better but then never get the privilege to pursue much of it after. Yet, it's not a waste. If there is anything that will remind you of your worth- it's when you set out to do something you are afraid to do and you nail it!

So our life was pretty much like any other single mom family trying to make ends meet with four kiddos'. She had a couple of jobs and juggled us around. Once I aced my permit, and my sweet Uncle bought me my first car I was able to help her. But before then, she took us everywhere. I had a job and animals to tend to at the school barn; not to mention that my siblings had extracurricular things as well. She was our personal Taxi. Never complained. She just did it. I never regretted moving to the little retirement community on the lake. Our life had flowed into this normalcy until April thirtieth nineteen nine-seven. Our life in that small town was good for us, even though we missed Dad. We missed all of our family down South, but we also adjusted pretty well. Moving on sometime is a necessity.

When Mom went to Prison our cute little house went back to the

Owner. My mom says that the Owner had been so kind to us, and never kicked us out when she couldn't pay rent. Memaw and I went and got the most valuable things from the house and put them in storage. We paid for the storage unit for a couple of years and then went and emptied it out with the things that we knew she would want. That was difficult to do. You're surrounded by all of these things that were once held by not only mom but my sister, loved by her and a reminder of our life. Even her own belongings. Things that were in our house during the time she was alive. It was hard to let some of them go for my mom's sake. To know that she would be sad that so much stuff would be gone, but there was no place for it and we could no longer afford to keep the storage unit. It was like we took a big eraser and wiped out what we had. Our life there.

Court and Court

Give all your worries and cares to God, for
He cares about what happens to you.
1 Peter 5:7

bout a year after my sister's murder, the trial for her murderer
started. My sister's murderer; my mom's ex. At that time I'm
nineteen and living with my boyfriend, while working at the
Airport. Let's stop here for a moment. After graduation, I decided to
give living near my dad and his wife a try, so I moved in with my dad's
sister-in-law and started waitressing at a hole in the wall cafe. I made
really decent money actually and enjoyed being close to my brothers
who both lived with my dad. Deep down inside though I missed my
mother, Memaw and my uncle. I missed the life we had. No doubt
that that was all gone yet I couldn't help but miss it all. Before the
first trial started I moved back to the area to move in with my long-
distance boyfriend that I had had for six months.

One of the things they usually do in cases that are covered largely
by the media is to move locations. It was moved to another city, which
was still another small country town. The truth is it wouldn't have

mattered where we moved to for trial; he was guilty. This was another challenging time in my life. Hard, hard stuff. These trials would keep me thin in size and mind. Everyday wrapped me up in nausea, and so little food touched my lips. Basically I lived on crackers and Gatorade. There was never an appetite for food or even water. Being so raw still, I couldn't think about much of anything else but what I had lost. Sometimes, life around me helped distract me. I coped with just keeping my eyes on the next thing for me to do in life. But it was different when it was in your face all the time and life couldn't appear normal. I lived with this awareness of fear suddenly. My everyday life appeared functioning but inside there was a darkness that hid in the corner of my heart. In that darkness my life could be ruled by anxiety that would overwhelm me at any point. The trial brought back the fact that life wasn't normal. I was overwhelmed emotionally for sure. The murderer had taken away my entire normalcy. Not just a person, my sweet sister, but my family. My mother, my brothers, it was all different and gone. I found it hard to be around others. Life seemed easier to plow through if it was done alone. I refused to sleep my life away but I did sit in front of the tv and consume my mind with comedy or cartoons.

If only I had reached out to others who may have helped me see things differently. Maybe if my mom had been free herself and not going through her own stuff we could have worked out this whole mess together. But my mom was locked up in jail on the very day of my high school graduation. Yes, the day I graduated from high school. My mom didn't see me graduate. I wanted to go sit with her in jail and skip graduation and all the other "family" that were able to attend. Seemed so hopeless. Pointless even. Oh, yes, so by the way, your sister is dead; your baby brother is still recovering and so now let's lock up your innocent mother. Less than a month after my sister's murder, my mother was put in jail. Then she was having to prepare her own defense after she was bailed out of jail, which was not immediate.

So back to the little town. The cute little town. My best friend and I went together, and neither of us remember a lot of the details. But her presence was much needed. She is like home to me. One of my few memories from then was that we ate at a restaurant on the square in downtown; it was a meeting with someone in Authority regarding the trial. The town seemed to be buzzing though. Media trucks with reporters were everywhere. Most of them didn't know who I was until after I testified. Thank goodness because I could walk around unscathed. Since they had no clue who I was I could watch all of the commotion pretty much while being left alone. The rule is that you can't sit in the courtroom until after you testify if your family, so that was mostly the whole trial. While waiting for my turn to testify I would go sit outside under a big tree on a cement courtyard that kept me calmer than being directly outside the court. The breeze would blow my hair and remind me to breathe. The calmness outside helped keep my insides calm, my spirit calm and my mind calm. God's beauty and creation complimenting each other.

My stomach was in constant knots knowing that I would have to be up on the stand soon. I'd have to look at him. Look at the man who killed my white-haired beautiful sister. It felt a bit like a dark cloud following me around. Waiting. Since I hadn't seen him before that trial, it stirred questions. There are plenty of days that I wish I could have asked him a question. Just one. And it's a one-word question too. One that every family member wants to ask the murderer. Why? But I couldn't and I never did and that will be regretful till eternity. Yet maybe he wasn't all that sure either. Maybe it was drugs or anger, or revenge. It doesn't matter. Finally, the DA called me to the stand to testify. I sat there and answered each of the questions that the Prosecutor asked me. I did my best to ignore him there. Looking so nonchalant but also the same that he always looked at me. Awkward and uncomfortable in his own skin. After being asked if the defendant was in the room; I had to point him out. I looked at him but I didn't want to look *into* his eyes or even stare at him long enough to gain any kind of emotion. I knew that if I fixed my eyes on his or even him I may have come unglued. So I saw him but I didn't really see him.

If you ask me, a blind rat could have prosecuted him and gotten a guilty verdict and the death penalty. There was never a question of whether he was guilty. I mean, he showed them where her body was. He then tried to blame his cousin for her death. We knew that he was the one who took her life and tried to take my baby brother's. My heart never cared too much about him dying long after on death row either. His life was over anyway. Prison was imminent though. They could have carried him out to the gallows that day and it wouldn't have made a difference to me. I wasn't an eye for an eye person. There is no bringing people back either way. It doesn't even bring closure nor take the sadness away. It doesn't bring anything that is tangible to me. Even after seeing a picture of my only sister's stabbed body at the crime scene.

That's what stuck out to me the most after his's trial. During closing arguments I was able to sit in the courtroom and watch. I regret that choice for a long time. A lot of stuff that the Prosecutor said about my mom wasn't true or kind. The picture he tried to paint was a lot of his opinion about my mother and me. Not true facts. What's sad is that he didn't know her. Or me. I understand he was just doing his job, but he judged her solely on the dirty house she kept and the fact that she was overweight. He judged her because we were poor. Yep, I just said that he judged us because we were poor, and not like him and his rich little estate he owns out in the country. If he had taken the time to really get to know my family, I doubt he would have felt so strongly against us. He still does, and even asked a friend of mine once if I was a "good mama?" Small town talk. But perception isn't always reality. Sure, we were poor, and my mom was a terrible housekeeper, but she would do anything for us.

During the closing arguments he put up the giant poster of my slain sister. Immediately I closed my eyes really tight. Tried to unsee it but it was too late. Her beautiful hair all around her as she lay lifeless. Barely clothed. My sweet little sister. The air left my body for a moment. It was one of those pictures that you don't want to keep. It was a picture that I didn't want to stay in mind. It hurt. Tore me right up. Sometimes after that day if I started to think about her I would close my eyes and see it. That awful picture. I could be driving and it would pop up. Her little body lying on the ground lifeless. All of those stab wounds. Her exceptional spirit gone. Desperately I wanted to unsee that poster, to unsee her like that, to unsee the evil that had occurred. After reading the Bible I got down on my knees and begged God to take the image from my mind. Make it lighter, make the impact lesser, just do something so that it wasn't so heavy. I believe that God did lessen the impact. Now, I just see white around all around. Her sweet face and her beautiful cotton top hair. Thank goodness because that was a hard picture to carry around in my soul.

On May twenty-eighth nineteen ninety-eight, the murderer got the death penalty and he was executed on December third two thousand nine. No one in "Authority" even notified me when he was up for execution. Maybe they felt like I didn't exist since I didn't seem to agree with the way they perceived my mom. On his execution date I had a two-month-old baby at home and wouldn't have left her anyway. Truth is by that time, I had found a new love and life in Christ, so I would have declined an invitation to go watch a man be put to death. Forgiveness with peace took over my life by then. By that time the only thing that concerned me was his salvation. Seemed off to watch someone die anyhow. My sister wouldn't pop up right after his last breath anyway, right? The only thing left for him from me was forgiveness and wondering if he had accepted Jesus as his Lord and Savior. If he had accepted him into his heart and life. Hopefully the good news was shared with him before he passed. I believe Hades deserves no one if it can be helped. That's why Jesus came to earth, remember? Even the man who raped and stabbed my sister to death can repent. If he was moved and convicted and made a new creature in Christ Jesus, then praise the Lord. If he believed in his heart Jesus is Lord and confessed with his mouth, then I will see him in Heaven. I am not the judge. I'm just a sister in Christ Jesus.

My Mom's trial was after his. Not long after either. Felt like another battle in the ring. Even to this day it's hard to believe that I went through all of that, three times. My sister's murder's trial, my mom's trial and then her appeal trial. Again the DA wanted me to be a major witness for him, and I was baffled. Each trial was still a media fest. In fact, while writing this book I've read plenty of articles that I wish I hadn't. Details that my heart doesn't want to relive. I get angry reading. Still Mom's trial was different for me, this time I felt persecuted along with her. Especially after I testified. I had not been the character witness that the Prosecutor had hoped for. Never in my wildest dreams did I think my mom heard something that night. My mom always did her best for us. After I testified, he turned on me as well. To hear the Prosecutor accuse me of being in on the crime. Like I literally wanted to punch him in the face. To say that my mom and I would have planned this, or that we would have in anyway harmed my siblings. Why? What was the reason any sane person would let a dirty man do all that he did to our babies? What a punch in the gut. Disbelief that this Prosecutor who told me in the murderer's 's trial that I would remind the jury of my sister, a good example of what she would be like had she not been murdered. That I was a future image of what was lost. That I would make her proud. But I was naive to the way *their* world worked. That lesson came at a big price for me because I didn't know if I could trust people in authority after that. Life wasn't so black and white. Never once has my heart or gut told me that Mom was negligent that night. So, it turned out that my testimony for him wasn't what he hoped. Leaving that stand afterwards I knew that I had conducted myself with integrity.

Again, there really wasn't any evidence to convict my mom. The State felt like there was no way that she could have slept through the murderer taking the kids in the early morning hours. They felt like she should have heard them scream. I know it sounds awful to even think otherwise, but that is what I believe happened. She lay sound asleep with a big box fan on her face because we had no heat or air. She was asleep. Even after the trial the Prosecutor said this in the newspaper *"Good mamas protect their children. Is she a good mom? No. She is the kind of person who puts her needs before her kids'. Her need was her boyfriend. We know that"* But apparently the Prosecutor didn't know that. Mom had kicked her boyfriend out a month before. She did not want him in our lives anymore. My mom had no indication that this tragedy would happen and she simply did not feel like he was mature or responsible enough for our family. She decided to break it off with him and he did not like that. So, sir … her need wasn't him. After she realized that he wasn't good for her family she kicked him out. Forgive me, but you still don't jump to the conclusion that your ex is the one who kidnapped your kids either. Remember, you never think anything bad will happen to you or your family. Ever. The newspaper clipping that I have now only angers me more because of the foolishness that is stated in them. My new experience with media outlets makes it tough for me to read articles about "true" stories or things that are happening in the news because it's probably not even half-truth. There is always more to the story and the people than you will hear. Good and bad.

During my mom's trial the Prosecutors brought in experts. They had experts on the stand to say you should be able to hear noise from this room to that room. It was all kinds of circumstantial. She says she never heard anything and I believe her. There have been a couple of mornings that I have woken up to FB posts talking about the tornado sirens going off and I never heard them. I slept right through the whole thing. That's really scary, to be sleeping so well that you don't hear sirens that could save your family's life. Yet, it does happen. But the media told mom's story from a negative standpoint. That her value and innocence was wrapped up in the fact that she was poor, single with four kids, a terrible housekeeper, and rumors of things she said but that she didn't. Have you ever been misunderstood? We were.

Also, another piece of evidence against her was that she apologized to my youngest brother at the hospital. She told him that she was sorry she didn't help him or save him from what the bad man did. This bothers me as well because now that I have kids and I have apologized to my children for things I had no control over. Not only something I had no control over but for something I wasn't even around for. It's kind of like guilt for not protecting your kids from every bad thing in the world. But let's be honest, that is life. That is the way the world is and even though our hearts are in the right place to make that apology, it's not our fault either. When my second daughter started Kindergarten a little Hispanic girl told her that her yellow hair was ugly. That she was ugly. My second daughter started to doubt even the clothes that she put on. I was so angry. I apologized to her because I don't want her to see the world as this angry thing that she's not good enough for. I apologized to her for something someone else did because *SHE* is my baby. I apologized to her because I wasn't there to stand up for her. Honestly, I didn't know what else to do for her and I needed my girl to move forward. Somehow, somehow I wanted her to figure out that the little girl was completely wrong and maybe she was hurting herself and so we should just ignore her. I apologized for something I had no control over. None. That is the closest thing I can compare what my mom did. She didn't apologize to him for hearing them and not acting on their behalf. She apologized because she didn't hear them. Had she had control over the situation.

My Mom's trial was also in a different town, a bigger town though than the cute little one of the murderer's. It was in a tall building and the courtroom was like on the third floor. The trial lasted a few days and on the day that we got the verdict in I was in the courtroom; it was October fifteenth. During this time we got to know her attorney better and spent as much time as possible with mom, just in case. There was this heavy looming feeling that this really could end with her going to Prison. It may not have made sense to us, but it was very well a possibility. My older brother, my Memaw, and I, we all sat together. My Mom sat at her table with her head in her hands. I was so done by this point, my body was thin, weak and I was just hanging on. There I sat next to my Irish twin with my head bowed. Waiting with my breath held for the verdict to be read. At first looking at mom made me feel worse. So I closed my eyes. Then I heard "Guilty." Injury to a child by omission, two counts. Twenty-three years in prison. I started to cry and my Irish twin stood up and walked out. I could hear a few sobs from others. I think my grandmother said something and the Judge ordered everyone to be quiet. I stood up. There was no air. I couldn't breathe and I had to get out of that room. Surely, surely I would wake up. As soon as I stepped outside the courtroom I sat on a bench in front of a window and I waited. Doing my best to stop the swirling and catch my breath. There was nothing in that courtroom I wanted to be a part of anymore. My world just collapsed even more. Looking out the window, the world looked as though nothing had happened in that courtroom. No indication that my whole world just changed again. Funny how something so horrible in your life is present and the world goes on. People walking around and laughing with each other. Frozen, I stood there watching the hustle of people out the window. People eating in the nearby restaurants. The cars pass by, like it's just a normal day. Life was going on out there, that's what life does though, it goes on. But my world stopped again.

Minutes later everyone filed out into the hall and out of the courtroom. Reporters, Bailiff, Prosecutors, and spectators. Then, there was Mom- last. Handcuffed with shackles on and red eyes with a hint of tears. There were reporters all around her trying to get something to show for the news. I looked at her and burst into tears. I just wanted to latch onto her and make the world go away. *Why couldn't the world just go away?* I couldn't believe this. *Why is this happening to us?* Yet when I looked up at her again, she looked strong and she said my name and she said, "head up, chin out, shoulders back." Then she gave me the "I love you" sign in sign language. It was her thing that she always did to us. With a heap of tears I replied, I love you Momma. The world paused for me a little. Slow motion almost. She stepped into the elevator. Officers on both sides of her and her attorney's. She again looked strong as she faced forward. My heart hurt so badly, and tears were flowing so freely so I put my head down and tried to gain composure. Reporters, family, friends, and people who we thought were friends but were all still out in the hallway discussing what just transpired. I looked up again and the doors were closed and she was gone. Just like that. If I didn't hate the world before, I really hated the world at that moment. I really wanted to run after her; just go with her wherever she was going I wanted to go. All over again life seemed scary, hurtful, and pointless. To me, if you could send that woman to Prison, you might as well send me. Send any mother whose child gets murdered or kidnapped from your own home, right?

It's a shame that our justice system is set up the way it is. They make mistakes. Innocent people go to prison and it's sad. It's a real shame that people can slander innocent people and it truly changes their fate. They can go to jail. They do go to jail. In fact, they go to prison too. I read the old clippings from all of that time and I am saddened by all the garbage that was spewed from different people. But what are you going to do to stop it? If I had known how to fight back at nineteen years old I would have. All I could do was be angry. Sometimes I did pray that tragedy like ours never came upon them. It's not as hard as you think it might be to pray for your enemies. It releases so much anger sometimes. You can breathe a little more. Like my Memaw said to a Reporter after the verdict, "May God forgive them." I pray nothing like what happened to us, happens to anyone. Even those involved in sending Mom to prison. Talk about out of control. Those times were out of our control. It didn't matter who they actually were. My mom is a good momma. Still the best momma and now grandma.

Mom was shipped off to the transition facility before she was placed into a permanent prison. Every chance I got to go see her; wherever I could go see her, I did. She was in prison for a couple of years and then she had an appeal trial. The media was around for that one too. Just not as bad and in your face, or as big, but they were still interested in her story. I was twenty-one at the time. Still lost and dazed. Still trying to cope with my loss by not being alone for any length of time. My boyfriend at the time attended the hearing with me.

The appeal wasn't a whole trial this time, just a hearing on adjusting her punishment. Mom was represented by a different Attorney this time. He was more seasoned for this type of work. This trial wasn't as long. Still a jury though, and at least I knew that it couldn't get worse. Waiting for the verdict in the courtroom during this appeal with Mom and my boyfriend was still hard. While the jury was deliberating the new punishment we were left in the courtroom. Just us and the guard. Well there was a group of people sitting in a spot I couldn't see. So I assumed it was just us and the guard. We talked quietly. Sat silent but then I sang for her. She asked me to sing, so I sang "Lord I Hope This Day is Good" and I meant every word of it. I wouldn't normally just bust out and sing like that in front of a stranger, but I did. I did it because she asked me too. My mom always believed I could do anything I wanted and one of those things was a singer. She begs me to sing sometimes.

We loved to sing as a family. Before mom's first trial I had auditioned at a place just because I wanted too. It was my passion and dream to sing, but that died with my sister. I think I auditioned in honor of my mom as well. They gave me great feedback, but singing was just something I could do but no longer something I dreamed of pursuing. Dreaming at all was dead to me. Although I have a signature that I practiced when I started middle school; I no longer dreamed of the stage. I love to worship and sing to God, lullabies, and anything else but the dream died. My kids and I sing in the car or in the house. If someone starts singing a song we all chime in, and my heart swells. I have been redeemed. I forget because of what my life looks like presently, but I HAVE been redeemed.

The jury came back with still bad news. In the end she still got eight years on two accounts for her punishment sentence. Crazy part is that one of the jurors, or a couple of them, said that they just wanted her to be in Prison until my youngest brother turned 18. Although she did get awarded visitation rights to see him before he turned eighteen while she was in Prison, so a lot of good that did. That was nice for her. Just to see her baby boy. I believe that he was ready to see her as well and I took him on his first visit to see her. I **IMAGINE** that a little healing happened then too for both. That those two needed to see each other for healing purposes. Think about the fact that the last time she saw him was in the hospital when she told him that she was sorry she didn't save him. That admission to something that wasn't a real admission. It wasn't a heavy or awkward meeting either. It was almost as if we hadn't missed a beat. The three of us.

Her attorney again appealed but she remained with that punishment. I knew her attorney was doing all that he could and so I never felt like she was under served or not taken care of by him or his office.

It was hard again leaving her there at the courthouse. Knowing she would go back to all of that mess that was a different life than what she knew, and definitely than what she deserved. I do remember thinking; well maybe this is God's plan for some things to get worked out within her. Maybe there was a greater plan in all this for her. I didn't know God the way I do now, so I wouldn't have blamed him. What I might have done was see the supernatural. But I held on to the idea that maybe it was for a reason. That was a good coping sentence I would repeat over and over. There must be a reason.

My Mom's in Prison

Trust me in your times of trouble,
And I will rescue,
And you will give me glory.
Psalm 50:15

After Mom's first trial she went to a temporary prison facility. It's not where she would stay; it was more like getting her in the system and figuring out where the space is for her to finish out her sentence. We had always seen her in regular jail. The glass you have to look through and the phone you have to talk in. But I wasn't sure what to expect with an actual Prison. My Memaw and I were her first visitors, of course. I barely slept the night before. I barely ate as well, but hey that's no surprise still then in my life. We drove together, my grandmother and me. We hardly stopped on our way up there. We just wanted to get there and see her. Seriously for two hours I was so nauseous I just wanted to throw up or turn around and head back home. Stopping only made this worse, therefore I only stopped once. My head felt like it was going to spin right off my shoulders. But we made it and we walked up and got our IDs checked and our body scanned and we walked into this room with tables everywhere and then the phone booth looking areas. It didn't feel like this should be a part of my life, a little nineteen-year-old and her grandmother visiting our loved one in Prison. Imagine being innocent and going to Prison for the first time. I bet that was even scarier, jail is bad but Prison is like a whole new world. There are murderers, thieves, I mean not a lot of people you would want to invite to your kid's birthday party.

Walking in I noticed a big area with lots of round tables, and then off to the side were big glasses with phones. We had to sit at the spots with the phones, which meant we didn't get to touch her still. It's been a long time at this point since I have touched my mom. Which meant hugging or anything, and typically I didn't care about that stuff. But I missed her. Talking into those phones is a punishment all on its own. Think about all of the conversations with tears and snot that have been shed into those phones. I don't care how many times they have been sprayed with Lysol; it wasn't enough. Memaw let me pick the phone up first and talk to her. I don't think I even knew what to begin with. Mom was already crying a little. Even I was a bit tender. Mixed emotions really. Happy to look into her eyes and see her. See no physical evidence of mistreatment. Hear her words, see her sappy tears as well. There was relief that at least I could see her and know that she was alive. We were able to buy her a soda and snacks, not that any of us could really eat much but it was the action of it. We visited her this way for nine months. Those visits were tough. We couldn't touch her and the conversation always felt bottled up. It made the visit heavier. But I was glad to do them. It was better than death. It was better than nothing. Finally she was moved to her permanent location. A place bigger and without the glass. Still an intimidating place for sure.

When we came to visit her the first time at the new place, it was a lot like the temp place. Your car had to be registered as a visitor, and then you walked up to the guard shack on the outside of these two huge fences. The guard shack checked your I.D.'s, gave you a heads up to the inside so that they could get the inmate you wanted to see, and then they use the wand to scan your body and check your dress code. The only time I was turned away was because I wore a wedding dress, but never made it past the guard shack. That was one of my less proud moments. I was marrying my second husband so this was my attempt at including her or at least letting her see me in a wedding dress. Unfortunately my attempt to include mom wasn't worth the price of me not getting to see her. It was a dumb idea. Really. Not to mention- that marriage was over before it began.

Once you made it past the outside guard, the guy in the tall tower would buzz you in through both gates one at a time. Then once you were inside they took your information again and the inmate's info and sat you down at either a table or a glass booth in another room. We got a table. The joy of a table! When the weather was nice you could even sit outside at a picnic table and that was always my favorite. We sat down at this round table and waited for Mom to walk in. The tables were like the lunch tables and chairs you would use at school. There were lots of other visitors waiting for their loved ones as well. Some were small children and infants with people who appeared to be Grandparents. Mom walked in and we both gave her this long hug, but not too long for fear of being reprimanded, but a hug. I am not a touchy-feely person. But the act of getting to hug her after so long was such an uplifting thing for me. The freedom and the absolute gift of it all! I was so thankful to touch her finally. There was no nasty phone to talk through or glass to look through. Just us. As soon as we sat down Memaw and Mom held hands. Which made me emotional to look at Memaw's fragile hands inside moms. Mom and daughter sitting together. We sat there and it was a little like winning the lottery. The three of us, three generations of women who were sharing something hard together. We bought sodas and snacks and had fellowship together in a new way. You know what they say about food and fellowship, and how well they go together. It was a two hour visit each time and so it took us a while to get over the queasy bellies and enjoy the snacks together. But soon we would find stuff we liked in the vending machine and hope it was there for our visit. Each month I lived for those visits. I don't think anyone around me understood that either. Aside from my mentor and Memaw. Leaving mom there never got easier but the actual visit got me through another month. Memaw and I would take turns sometimes and then go together on special occasions. They would take pictures for us too that we would buy to keep or share. I had collected a lot of them and mom brought them home with her when she was released. We mainly bought them and she would get to take it back to her cell. Our lives were definitely different. So these pictures were reminders that there would be another visit soon. Mom in Prison, Memaw and I visiting every month, my brothers living a few hours away with Dad. I think we all had this different way of getting used to our lives.

There were times I wondered and sometimes still do today if she had paused her grief. If her time in Prison was like a pause button on grieving? She went from her daughter murdered and son left for dead to fighting for her life to remain outside of Prison. Was there time for grief or was it stifled? I'm not sure how you can heal if you don't have time to process your pain. Certainly I could not have done it like she did. If she did. Grief is a process; so to go from loss to surviving seems so cruel to me. Especially concerning my momma. The momma who would give you her last dollar. Give me her last anything.

My Sins

There is not a single person in all the earth
who is always good and never sins.
Ecclesiastes 7:20

Right before Mom's trial I had met a cute guy. It all starts with meeting a guy it seems. It felt like I was in love with him instantly. But I moved away and we started a long-distance relationship for a few months. My guy and I kept our relationship going but it was getting harder. Since I wasn't sure about college, I worked as a waitress at a hole in the wall place and lived from day to day. It didn't take but about six months before I moved in with my boyfriend. Boyfriend convinced me that we were meant to be together, and I really believed it. I had saved myself till him, at nineteen years old. Right away we got pregnant because well, that's what happens when you play that game; you can conceive a baby. Shocker. Which was my whole reason for keeping my virginity so long. Babies. His reaction was to get married because he and his family were very religious. Sometimes religious people create religious bondage. After discussing with his family we planned a decent size wedding for the Fall of ninety-eight, right about after Mom's trial. Our relationship was still good but I was starting to notice how he treated me and I wondered if this was the right thing to do. He was an Army kid; he himself was in the Army. Often we would travel to see his family and friends whom he was close with. They were a good family.

Since he worked nights mostly he would be sleeping when I got home from work after five. Our lives just trucked on. Most of the time I felt consumed with Mom's pending trial and planning a wedding. I kept myself busy, even maybe ignoring my second thoughts. That was me it seemed; I would just go along with things with no real grip of what I was really getting myself into. I didn't like rocking the boat then. Or maybe it was just naive. One day I had noticed spotting while at work but the Nurse calmed me down and told me to rest with my feet up and call back if it got worse. That night it got worse and worse and it was time to go to the hospital. I let him know what was going on and he was annoyed then. But once I woke him up to leave he was so angry at me. Even lashed out a bit as if I were making something up. He told me I was overreacting and made me feel stupid. All of a sudden I felt alone. He was angry at me, while I am scared to death and bleeding everywhere. While I am potentially losing his child he is mad at me? Finally we left for the hospital. Trash bags on the seat, me sitting there so nervous and terrified that I would lose the baby.

By the time we arrived the baby was gone. There I am sitting on the hospital bed throwing up. I would need to abort my baby who had passed away. The only comforting person in that room was my OBGYN. Shortly after that my mom showed up to the hospital to be with me for the D and C. My fiancé gladly went home so that he could go to work. There was no, "Hey, I'm sorry, I want to be here with you" not an ounce of sadness. I didn't even feel love from him. There was my second clue that something with us wasn't right. There I was losing our baby and his actions told me that he cared less. He was disconnected from me and from what was happening to us. It was a hard time for my mom and me. When I think about it, I can see us there in the hospital room together after the D and C. She was sitting on my right side. We were sad but there was peace. She stayed as late as they would let her. She gave me the strength I needed to go through this loss. Here we were facing something hard together yet her fate was wearier on me than my reason for being in the hospital bed. Miscarrying broke my heart. My heart felt heavy for losing something so precious but I knew that I would be ok. Something about the way he treated me told me that the story may take a different turn. Less than a month after that was her first trial and she went to Prison. Of course she didn't attend the wedding. The wedding that should never have happened. After I lost the baby Mr. Wrong started mistreating me as if I was broken to him. Not sure how you go from being so in love with someone that you convince them to move back to your city, shower them with gifts and love - to just pure hate for them. Our time courting together wasn't imaginary, but it wasn't lasting love. It was obvious by his slap on my face that he was not in love with me. There were more and more days of belittling with hatred towards me. He said to me once in the kitchen "If you ever become anything it will be because you wanted to prove you were something to me; it will be because you wanted to prove me wrong." Boy did he make it easy to walk out. Mostly there was remorse for all the love I tried to give him. But the way he talked down to me and made me feel about myself was awful. The words were worse than the physical. Here I was this lost, hurting young girl already and he just stomped on my heart. Mental and physical abuse is wrong and it is not love. It is someone trying to control you, and I was never anyone's property.

There is no regret about that part of my life OR any part because

it is what it is. It made me more aware and it showed me how strong
I was. Although I can't say I grew out of being naive and agreeable
because sometimes I can be the latter too much. Still struggling to
be alone but I didn't need hand holding through life. Also, I knew
that I wasn't about to be a victim of domestic violence. My parents
deserved for me to be courageous. It also gave me a glimpse of what
religious bondage is. Yes I was pregnant but I never thought that
getting married was the only option. But the fear of what others
would think pushed us to that decision. His parent's said it was the
only right way. If we had waited two more months there would not
have been a wedding. Because fear made our decision, and it was
costly. To his parents and to myself since it left a mental scar. I moved
what I had to my Memaw's house and moved right on with my life.
The divorce was simple so my mentor and I handled it since at that
time I worked as her legal assistant. He got the house and everything
in it; I got my freedom and my self-worth. Oh, and our puppy. That
was plenty.

Family got redefined for me a couple of times since my parents'
divorce and my family crash. It kept looking different which is just
life sometimes. Here I was wondering what to do. No future planned
out, no real direction. My friend and mentor had taken me under her
wings a bit before my first divorce. She asked me to work for her as a
legal assistant at her office. This felt so great, maybe even purposeful,
yet nervous that I would fail at it. I knew that I would be out of my
league but she was willing to take a chance on me. The only thing that
was certain was my desire to make a difference and I thought that
this might be the way to do it. No college education or even knowing
where to start. But indecisiveness led me to think that my life would
be meaningless. Working in family law became hard on the heart.
Watching things that felt like injustice to me and I couldn't bear it
for very long. My skin was too thin and my heart lies to loose on my

sleeve. But in that time my friend and her family became family to me. Everything to me. She took such great care of me, which I will never be able to repay her for. She was my rock, my mentor, my second mom, my friend- she was just about everything to me. I think with all the crazy decisions I made I might have slapped me around a bit, but she never did. Just kept being there for me. She just kept on loving me through all of my poor choices. Everyone needs someone like her in their life, even if it's just for a bit. People like that help you stand and they keep "shooing" you in front of them. Kind of like, "I'm right here, I'm gonna watch you, make sure you're ok, but shoo." I plan on loving her forever. She may not have led me to Jesus, but she helped me live. She helped me keep choosing to live.

After a very short time single, I started dating a man that was over twelve years older than me. He approached me at the Nursing home we worked at and after our first date, it didn't take me long to move in with him. This relationship became one of the only ones that lasted longer than one year. There was a new house bought, new furniture, and memories made with his two children. His world brought a lot of drama from ex-wife for my phlegmatic personality. She was horribly mean to me and would call me names in front of the children, and I was too young for that. Defiantly too young to be with someone that much older with children. But he was also highly jealous and truthfully he had a right to be. After starting a new job at a manufacturing job I began flirting with a coworker. We met for coffee after work and started having a platonic relationship. It wasn't long before I started to believe that my future with my current boyfriend, who had given me so much, wasn't really who I wanted to be with long term. Soon enough the co-worker helped talk me into moving out and getting my own place. So I decided that I would just move out. He didn't deserve for me to up and leave, but I was afraid I could never have a peaceful life and my own children one day. Even if my intention was to leave my two-year relationship, my regret is that there was a thin line of adultery. Apparently I was a slow learner when it came to relationships. Oh to have a time machine. I wish I could tell my younger self, just relax, and give yourself a break. Stop trying too NOT be single or alone. Stop trying to fill a void. Please stop trying to get a new family. It won't dull the heartache.

There were wedding bells with the third guy who had been the co-worker, even after leaving him twice before because I didn't know what else to do. He was ten years older than me but he had two of the sweetest little girls. I think God was trying to get my attention which was why I left twice, but broken people only hinder other broken people. Third, Mr. Wrong was newly divorced. His ex-wife had left him, so maybe he was still hurting. I married him anyway. But I was still just running around this mountain, nearly naked, screaming "What do I do"? Needless to say, less than 6 months later I left him as well. Got my stuff and left after finding my own apartment. I had a new job in a different city and I felt like I should just jump and run. So I did. There was guilt leaving someone who only wanted to love me. Yet, I knew I couldn't get caught up in being a people pleaser. My heart hurt leaving those two sweets girls and confusing them. But again, I was a broken mess. The right thing to do was to leave. Besides, at my work I had started flirting with another co-worker, which turned into a kiss one time. Now I had become an adulteress in a whole new way. I knew after a couple of months of marriage that it wasn't going to last which is why I strayed, but still wasn't right. I felt like such an idiot. Again, just trying to fill in this hole left in my heart.

During this time, God had tapped me on the shoulder again in the presence of a sweet woman from my work who was a Christ follower through and through. Thank goodness it was a woman! Right? I listened to her and wanted her peace. Since I worked alongside her there was plenty of opportunity to ask her questions. That was the beginning of the end for my second marriage. I read a book by John Eldredge called Sacred Romance and began to go to church here and there with another friend of mine. Since my third Mr. Wrong wasn't interested in God and he also wasn't interested in having more children at the time; I felt trapped. But again, I left. Moved out and into my own place with a roommate. Finally on my own, life felt free. Things were changing, even I was changing.

Of course my self-image was really low because of the failed relationships. After a couple of weeks, I finally bought my first Bible. My life started with a bright orange metal Bible that contained the words that set me free. That unleashed a love that I had never known before. God makes beautiful things out of dust and dirt. Which thank goodness because I was a 'pro" outta making things dirty.

While waiting to divorce my second husband, I met my third ex-husband out at a bar. Yes, you read that right. So many ways I'd like to change my past. But then I promise you I would not have my four beautiful children nor would I be who I am today. I loved my kid's father very much. For sure I thought I could help change him and make him more like me, but that never happened. Now, my sweet kiddos pay the biggest price because they do not understand relationships or adult things. After twelve years of marriage, I could no longer go on. I once told someone that I would rather dig myself a grave and hop in it. I won't go into detail, but I know that I failed him. Just like he failed me. I wasn't an adulteress-I just felt abandoned and second class to someone who vowed to be my partner. The thing is we were so different even from the beginning and it didn't help. But as I look back, we should have waited more than nine months before getting married. The ink was still wet from my second divorce when he and I decided to get married, and I wish I hadn't. I had just found Jesus and I wish that that had been enough for me at that time. Yet, in those twelve years my love or my focus on Jesus never changed or waivered. I clung to him, prayed fiercely for help and wisdom during the last five to six years of marriage especially. My life wasn't what it seemed. Free will is real. Everyone has it. If we didn't then Jesus would not have needed to come to Earth. In saying that, people choose who they are. It's called free will for a reason. My then husband at the time was who he was and I couldn't make him choose things that I didn't like. I saw red flags but chose to ignore them.

My past, all of it; the three marriages, and the one engagement; like my sister's murder does not define me. Those six years of running around my mountain half alive screaming was a lot like the Israelites. I kept moving around this mountain thinking maybe that that was what I was supposed to do. Grumbling and lost all the while. God kept pursuing me anyhow. Just like the Israelites, I refused to listen to Him. The Mighty One calling my name, I kept flubbing it all up even though my intentions were well meaning. I was lost. People get lost; it's as simple as that. When I was young I fell in love with looking at the moon and writing short poems. Looking out my window would bring me hope for my chaotic and sad mess. It started to give me solitude in life. I could escape the mess all around me that the adults were going through. But also, I would look up and feel loved, just like someone up there could see me. So I learned to get stuff out of my soul by writing it down. I wrote this poem in all my darkness, during my mountain climb.

> They walk by
> Yet they see no tears
> They hear me speak
> My face never changes
> Always keeping it clear
> No emotion to detect

Can't see my heart with the sear
Heaviness in my spirit
No waking it in time
I just want to jump
Reclaim this life of mine
Pain made me weary
Keeps me in a bind
Listen with your heart
For me you may find

I'm thankful that I decided to keep climbing even though I didn't know where I was going. Those times kept me from maybe getting a different kind of lost. A loss that I might not have come back from. Sure, anyone can come out of anything. I know that firsthand. I did reach the top of that mountain, and looked over at the valley's I got caught up in. It's not the mountain that tripped me up. It was the refusal to listen to God. It was the refusal to stop and breathe. BE STILL. For me my idea of moving on was to create what I lost, but I was causing greater pain, causing just more sin in my life. Creating this self-image of myself that made me feel unworthy of anything great. I don't regret the mountain too greatly because I am so grateful now. I made a mess but now I can tell you to your face that you can get out of a mess as well. I have done it. Not alone, but I did have the courage to try. I became a new creation. The last twenty fours years I did my best to prove my life had been redeemed. That God had answered all of my prayers, but guess what, sometimes he just doesn't. Sometimes we decide what we want and we go after it and it's not what we need which can lead to a mess we create. Is it our fault? Yes. Can you feel immense guilt afterwards for it? Yes. Should you remember that you are loved and ultimately forgiven? Please, yes. Doesn't lessen the scar or hurt. But I didn't feel condemned for leaving my third husband since he and God know why. God knew my heart, heard my many prayers, witnessed every tear, and he also knows that I obeyed when asked. Only because of Jesus does my peace, joy and love look like it does. My life isn't all bad. Thank you Jesus.

The Orange
Metal Book

*Ephesians 2:8 God saved you by his special
favor when you believed. And you can't take
credit for that; it is a gift from God.*

My bright orange metal Bible was for teenagers, but I could
read it and understand it. It went straight to my heart.
The words came alive to me, just straight off of the
thin fragile paper. After being so exhausted from being lost and
trying to figure it out on my own I started to read it. It didn't just
stop at my brain either. My Heavenly Father had been calling me,
beckoning me for a while. Sweetly and gently drawing me to the
cross. Yet I kept getting married to everyone else but Him. I mean
in a way I kept saying *Sure*, but I thought I was good. You know,
well enough. That because I was a nice person, that that was good
enough. That each relationship I found myself in I thought was what
I needed to get through all the pain I was in. I didn't understand

that God was trying to free me. I needed to sit and be still and read His word. I was twenty-five years old, but I felt twenty years older emotionally. That was partly my fault for doing life without any sort of compass. So there I sat reading and crying. Just being broken in such a way that I was opened. Thank goodness I started from the beginning. The friend who I was going to church with told me to start with John. But I wanted to start at Genesis. The beginning. No confusion needed at what happened first. At the time, I worked at a manufacturing company as a receptionist so I could read while I answered the phones. I would be sobbing and have to compose myself before picking up the phone to greet the person on the other line. Sometimes I would ask a couple of the Christian co-workers a question or two about whatever it was I was reading at the time. I read every second I could. After work I would sit on my couch and read more. It took me less than 2 months to finish it. I was overcome with so many different emotions. It was and still is more than just a book to me. It has drama, lust, criminal justice, love, mystery even, underdog stories, and people doing God's work who would in no other way have the right to do so. Basically everything you need in an absolute great book! Truth is God has written all the greatest stories. From love stories to underdog stories and even stories about undeserving people being used to carry out big plans for Him. Most of my tears were not out of feeling outcast or judged but because I was moved. The overwhelming sense of the Holy Spirit was there with me. Also though, I felt very undeserving of his love. I felt Him over me while reading and I could not put it down. When I was reading it I wanted to touch Heaven. I was moved with anger and joy and mostly healing. Angry with shame at my own poor sin. Angry at the Israelites' for not loving God. Sad for God. I felt sad for Him because He loved His people so much and they just kept not loving Him back. For I had fallen in love. How could these people who were actually witnessing and "walking" with Him not love Him? I did and I only read about him!! Then I read about Jesus. Heaps of emotions came every time I would think about Him. I didn't remember the story of Jesus like what was in the Bible. The real story of him, not the Christmas version. Let's be honest, that doesn't give you much to fall in love with or know really much about. So when I read how He died for me on the cross, my goodness, the hole in my heart was closing up. My heart was so full and grateful at the same time. I have never and will never experience someone who loves me that much. Someone who knows that I am sinful and will sin on purpose and still be beaten to near death, then hung by hands and feet on a cross, then asks Abba, God, to forgive me because I don't have a clue, and then die so that it will be finished. So that I at least get a shot at Heaven. He is our only shot. I know that sounds kind of silly and simple, but it is. We have free will, but Jesus made the way for us. And if you ever read the Bible before, you know that you get to read a few different accounts of it from Christ disciples. So each time was still the same tears of healing. How can you not be healed once you read the New Testament? Even if you just start at John like suggested to me and read that part of the Bible, it will change you. My healing came.

All of a sudden the Christmas songs made sense and had new meaning to me. Song's I had been singing word by word literally like became new to me. I remember that first Christmas and crying when I sang Silent Night. I knew what it was really about. Or the song "Night Divine" the line "Till He appeared and the world felt it's worth," I felt that in my bones: my soul finally felt worth. The songwriters made the Bible come to life. The Bible never left my side until every page was consumed. Every page was setting me free. Each page was bringing me new hope. New joy and revelation about what I could do and be. Certainly there were things that made me ashamed.

But I really had no idea what I was doing when I was doing those things from my past. Not really. Except for doing my best to grow up and get a new family. I was trying to NOT feel alone. Doing my best to run from the darkness. Reading the good book was my start. Finally my soul felt loved and free. The loneliness never overtook me anymore. The presence of the Lord was with me, and the loneliness was almost completely gone. Forgiveness freed me as well. Even the man who murdered my sister. That whole forgiveness thing really isn't for the other person, it really is for your sake. Like forgiving my dad, and myself. My Dad because he isn't always what I want him to be. No other human can fill you or complete you. I didn't know that before so I kept getting bitter and hurt. Forgiving myself because in a sense I had let myself down by doing all these things that were making me lose ground. I had hurt others in the process of all my listless wandering. My half clothed run up the mountain screaming really hurt those who tried to love me and complete me. But I am human as well, and I sin and will keep sinning, but I do know that I don't want to.

My relationship with Christ has transformed me. It actually felt a lot like coming home. And for a girl who moved so frequently, home were really just people. Like my grandma was home to me my whole childhood, until I reached fourteen. After that it was just different loved ones, and even someone who wasn't my blood. Finding God made me feel free and whole. For years after my sister's murder and mom incarceration I felt a whispering from Him. My life turned upside down and I was just trying to zip through it. Get married, have something to look forward to. Make no mistake, it might make sense trying to cover up my sin or fleshiness with a good excuse of all my pain. My tragedy was a great reason to remain a victim. My sin was adultery, and sexual immorality. Sin doesn't have to be labeled good, bad, or worse. Sin is sin. But you can leave the darkness and your fleshy ick once you see the light. Once you meet the Light. All you have to do is keep walking towards it. You don't have to be perfect or sinless, you just have to open your heart and say yes to God.

My mountain and suffering have brought with it a great deal of understanding and peace after my inside transformation. It basically left me wide open to receive healing and to give forgiveness away. Receive Jesus wholeheartedly. I had been so angry at God once. I wrestled with him at the picnic table. Blaming Him and not understanding why. There was no faith in my foundation so I crumbled. I was not raised with that, to believe in the strength God gives you. Even now, many years later I need no one's acceptance. I need no strength or grace that comes from anywhere but God's. There are plenty of times I get discouraged or have my heart hurt by people I love, but I know where to go. Where to start now. Even when the worldly views try to creep in. And you know what I mean. They say: You need a bigger house; your car is not as nice as so and so's; or why aren't you going on a nice family vacation? Or, hey you should buy some cuter clothes; or hey I thought so and so was your friend? How about gossip? The list just goes and goes. It's a tricky place to be or stay. Even loneliness tries to creep in. There is a whisper from Satan that says, you are not seen, or heard. You are not needed. You are alone and everyone else has all of these great relationships with other great women, but you don't. You are unworthy. Yet, my Redeemer lives and reminds me of all that I do have. The goodness of his love and mercy. I find rest there. Rest knowing that that is all that I really need. My desire is to remain an ambassador for Christ and give Him all the glory, so I can't sit around and gnash my teeth about the finances I don't have for dance class for my girls. Nor should I grumble at any other first world problems I may have. There were plenty of days when I would rather drive off the bridge and leave this world behind. I'm pretty sure Mom felt this way too. My thoughts would go to her when despair had me in a pit. Imagining her there in Prison all alone with strangers. I couldn't leave her. She had already lost so much. So I would write and get it off my chest. I wrote this poem during my really dark days.

> It is here,
> I thought it was gone.
> Thought it died
> But it crept in slow
> Pushing it nowhere
> They never fill it
> Always come near me
> Why can't they see
> No joy in my voice
> This is not who I am
> Pain still lingers
> Now I don't care
> Tired of the anger
> Tired of pain
> Can't make it stop
> It seems to stay
> Why can't I disappear?
> I'm ready for my Maker
> I'm tired of it here.

There were plenty of days I wanted to die. Lord it would have been so much easier to not be here on Earth. Maybe also, I felt undeserving of a good life. Sometimes we think Jesus is much too good for us. The scripture Luke 5:1-11 gives me a good point for this. Simon says to

Jesus "Go away from me, Lord; for I am a sinful man." Jesus had given him specific instruction and Simon obeyed, even reluctantly and he was rewarded with this overflow of fish. I felt undeserving. But also it reminds me that sometimes we are so lost and caught up in so much fleshy stuff that we don't want to get Jesus dirty with our problems. With our sin. Messed up in our own dirt. But then Jesus says, "Do not be afraid, for now you will be catching men." Now what does that mean, right? That even though I am a sinful man, I can fish for men. I can be used. I am not as dirty or broken as I think. Or even useless. He says just turn away from the dirt. Tend the harvest with me. I am here, do not be afraid. I will guide you. The scripture Matthew 4:19 says "Come, follow me," Jesus said, "and I will send you out to fish for people." Now doesn't that feel more like a reward? For most of us an undeserved reward. It gives you a purpose too or for some of us a race to run. But that is what Jesus was all about. He needs you to stop being all about you, your sin. Just turn from it. Or forget it maybe and get out of your own mind. Go serve someone. In fact maybe he needs you a little dirty so that you can be less judgmental and more open. What if overcoming your mess is a tool to help someone else. Be the light. For sure once you are doing kingdom work, big or small, your life feels more deserving. You tend to not have as many pity parties about whatever it is you think your life is missing. Or whatever you think your consequences of sin is keeping you from. Only one person was perfect and He died for us. There are plenty of sinful people in the Bible that God used because Jesus wasn't meant to be unattainable. God wants a relationship with you and then He wants you to share the Good News! At least this is all I have learned on the last many years; I feel like it's what God has shown me.

While at trial for my mom a man made her a purple cross. A total stranger, whom I will never know the name of. It was made with a satin rich purple ribbon that was threaded through the holes to make a cross. She kept it during her trial. But when she was sentenced to Prison, I found it and it became mine. I kept it in my car hanging from my mirror for a very long time. I would look up at it and think of her. Having it was a reminder of her strength, but also how one person made her a gift. A complete stranger made her a gift. Infact someone who might have believed like me, in her innocence. I didn't realize the true extent of what that gift would come to mean to me. What that purple cross was symbol of. I carried that cross with me for years but it wasn't for a while before I came to find it symbolic. How Jesus died on a cross for me. For you. My Mom has been home since two thousand and five and I still have it. You can generally find it in the current book I am reading or my Bible. One time my son had it in his little toddler hands and wielded it like a weapon. I held it in his little hands and told him that it was Momma's special cross. It's survived a long time in my care. It's a great reminder that I need Christ every day but also one of remembrance. That His grace is more than abundant for us all. That I may have gotten through some pretty rough stuff without the whole story but that maybe He was right there beside me and I didn't know. I didn't realize that He knew my journey would be tough and He was heartbroken for me. Wanting my heart to search Him out so that I could find freedom. I may not be going through something as intense or hard as losing my sister or difficult trials but I still need Christ. Every day I seek Him out and I find Him in His Words, because I am still growing. I think if you breathe air, life can be tough, but if you walk with Christ you can have it all- love, joy, peace, patience, kindness, goodness, gentleness, faithfulness, and self-control. Like many people, sometimes I wonder what my purpose is. Sometimes I let Satan whisper the lie that I am not enough. That I will never ever be enough and that life is just me cleaning in circles around my four blondes. That's why I have to step aside and meditate on Jesus. I have even let Satan tell me that I can no longer be used to serve God because of my last divorce. I am damaged goods. Just a big fat failure who should be only ashamed. But lo and behold I am reminded that I am loved enough to die for. Literally. So, then the world can have all it wants. Satan can whisper all he wants to me. But I am only concerned with what God thinks of me. It tells us in the Bible that seeking man's approval will only hinder our purpose in being a servant of Christ. Or you can read Galatians 1:10, it's a pretty great pressure relief valve on life.

My Mom's Last Day

Standing on the mountain top
Looking just how far we've come
Knowing that for every step
You were with us, Never Once
– Matt Redman

I t was such an anticipated day. One we dreamed about for years. We never knew when it would come and truth be told they didn't give us too much warning when it did. I wrote numerous letters each time her parole came up but it was never good enough. Once an inmate gets Paroled, they get to come home and live on probation until Probation Officer decides otherwise. There are certain stipulations and requirements they must follow. Each time we mailed out a packet to the Parole Board was nerve wracking. There was so much that had to be done and done correctly. I was by no means this fabulous conveyor of words. It was a lot of pressure to say the things that made the difference to release her. My friend and mentor at the time helped me by guiding me with all the proper guidelines. I wrote two different times to the Parole Board. You never go to speak with them in person, thank goodness because I might not have made it. The kind of person my mom was in prison was a bigger deal. If she was this horrible inmate always getting into trouble, it wouldn't have mattered what I wrote. I laugh at that because my mom is practically a saint. She would give anyone her last dollar if they needed it. She's not a pushover either, but she is kind and compassionate. Once at a business conference, a speaker said that if you have compassion for others that you have almost all you need to have a purposeful life. My mom has that licked, might just be where I get this unending desire to help. I see it in my girls too. It's hard to teach compassion, it's best served when it comes straight from your soul.

My first set of letters mailed off in December of two thousand, and then again in December two thousand three. But I didn't know she would be coming home in March of two thousand five. The day we drove to pick her up is in my top five favorite moments in my life so far. The giggles and tears from that day are stuck in my soul. We drove down to the Prison in my mom's best friend's pickup truck. My Mom has known her bestie since they were like fourteen years old. We call her aunt and we spent a lot of time with her and her family. It was her best friend and her husband, Memaw and me all stuffed in the truck. It's not like you imagine in the movies. You don't get to walk up and help them with their bags and hug. There was actually a small line of cars there to pick up their loved ones as well. Seems like they sent a few inmates home on the same day so there were other cars lined up and excited I'm sure just like us. She literally ran out to the truck. Threw her belongings in the back of the bed and jumped in the seat with us. We kept driving as directed, they didn't want anyone stopping for any reason. Just get your inmate and go! I remember her saying "Let's get as far away from here as possible." She was so- all of us- we were so hysterically happy that she was with us. Safe and sound. Loved. She was no longer their property. She was ours again! I thought I was going to explode. Sitting next to her in the truck I couldn't stop smiling. All teary eyed because my joy was overwhelming. While she was talking to us about how the process of leaving was and how it all went, I kept staring. There was complete awe that it was finally happening, so I was there soaking up the moment. My Momma going home was real finally. It was a new day for her. Well, it was a new day for me. Another new beginning for us. We headed to the next town to stop at the first Wendy's we saw off the highway. She needed to change out of her white prison jumpsuit and maybe try to grab something to eat. Really I just wanted to get back home. I almost hated to stop but we did, thankfully not for that long. Again, I couldn't eat or drink! So we all piled out of the truck giving her hugs with big laughter! I bet people were wondering what we were doing. Watching her go in and her come out in different clothes. For sure I know that if you were watching us you had to notice the joy in our conversation. The difference in just an everyday encounter with friends. Selfishly I wanted to get her home so she could rest! Not the sleeping kind of rest though. Rest in knowing that she would again have life. That not all was lost because of a group of strangers' judgment and misperception of her. Because of a system that unfortunately fails. How attorneys and others twisted things and made lies their truth. I know they had doubts but it wasn't our reality.

We planned for a small gathering at a crab food place that is kind of popular that same night. Later that night we met up there to kind of celebrate her coming home. Mom loves that place, and still does. Everyone that loved her and could be there, was there. I don't think any of us wanted to leave. We had another actual party for her later, a big barbecue at her best friend's house. After our dinner, I went home to my apartment and Mom went home to her first night under a house roof and not behind bars. I had kind of wanted to spend the night with her. Keep guard or something to make sure she was ok. It was a big sigh of relief that she was home again. But also, I couldn't believe that she was home and that part of our life was suddenly over. No more long drives that would keep me twisted till I got back home that night. There would be no more pat downs and barbed wire gates. Polaroid pictures of her in white would no longer be taken or needed. There wouldn't be a need for change for snacks or drinks. No more sad goodbye that left us aching each time. It was over. Just like that.

Coming Back

You keep track of all my sorrows.
You have collected all my tears in your bottle.
You have recorded each one in your book.
Psalm 56:8

The first time I had to come back to see a great friend of mine, I cried a bit. I lost a whole lot there in that town. I don't hate the town I graduated High School from; but for a bit of time I felt as though the town did a great job at messing with my life. It was the longest place as a kid I had ever lived. Three years was a lot to me, since we never seemed to stay anywhere long. When people ask me where I am from, I always laugh. How do you say nowhere really? But I graduated there and I lost the most I have ever lost there? Just there long enough that it changed my life. It is a great little town to grow up in. I loved that place. The country and small-town feel. I'm not sure about now since so much has changed but it used to be that everyone who was anyone knew something about someone. I wanted to live in a town like that so badly. Now my children and I live thirty minutes from the small town in another small town.

It used to be hard to visit the town I lost my sister in, but now it's just fuel for the memories. Like when I go over the first bridge into town; I see myself walking it with friends in the dark calling her name. My emotions of being scared sometime catch me as I recall that night. Calling her name, telling her it was ok. Hearing the water lap up by the shore. As you keep driving you drive past the City Beach, which now looks a bit different than when we were there. We spent so many days there swimming together as a family. I can see her there running around laughing, smiling so big you don't need the sun to see. Watching her and cautioning my brother to be careful in the deep. Those two together played like the best of friends. Fought as well, but they played more. My last two kids which is a boy and girl remind me of that- the playing and wrestling and then the sticking together. We had a lot of fun together as a family on the beach. Friends would meet us and we would spend hours there. If you keep driving you hit the town square. That place brings not so great memories. Believing a snake had my best interest at heart. For a long time I would picture my mom handcuffed being led away from there which I have a picture of from "County" News. There are good ones too though. We would go for ice cream at the parlor and Mom worked at one of the shops there part time so we spent quite a bit of time there on the square. We did the Christmas lights parade of homes and I'll never forget that. It was so beautiful at night. It was a place to be proud of. It still is. Go past both stop signs and keep going until the old school building on your right. The Field is there that she and my little brother would cheer and play football. I see her there with big blue eyes and so beautiful in her cheerleading outfit. Her pom poms up in the air and looking at us in the stands. They also held a Memorial there for her. I spoke there but I don't remember what exactly I said. There seemed to be a lot of people there to honor her. We were so thankful to those who knew us, really knew us, and her and supported us. We released a bunch of red balloons because red was her favorite color.

My sister loved butterflies, but we couldn't afford to release them due to the expense. In fact, when Mom encounters a nosy butterfly it makes her think of her. As if it's her way of saying "Hello". Sometimes I think of it that way too. In fact one day when my second daughter was like eight said "Mommy I saw Auntie yesterday" so I asked her what she meant. She said, "I saw her out in the yard, she flew right by me a few times saying Hi!" I love that she thinks about her and she has only met her in our conversations. She has only met her in my pictures. At first I thought maybe she meant she saw her in a dream. I used to see my sister in my dreams. But that has been such a long time ago. She would be there asleep. It was so odd to me and so real. Vividly she looked impeccable, peacefully sleeping like Sleeping Beauty. Like nothing had happened, as though she was just getting in a nap. My heart would be racing in the morning after one of those dreams. I wanted so badly to go back to sleep and see her. Just see her. It was ok that she was sleeping safe and sound. She never appeared to me any other way really. Many times I would lay there in my bed with my eyes closed praying to drift back to sleep and see her. Begging God to see her. I loved those dreams really because even though we were not interacting, at least she was safe there. It felt real to me. The closest thing to seeing her.

Then there is the Dairy Queen right next to the old school. Sadly it's an Italian restaurant now so it has changed so much. But when I pass by that place even though it's not Dairy Queen anymore, I see my lil' sister there walking up to me, in my memory. My Senior year I would pick her up after school and she would be there waiting for me. She went to tutoring and I told Mom I would get her when I got out of school. Every single time, I mean every single time, she would see me come in the door and run towards me. Run at me with her big, dimpled smile and hug me so hard. I hate to say this because it sounds so cruel but it annoyed me. Public displays of affection made me uncomfortable. Reluctantly I would hug her back and be annoyed that she acted like she hadn't seen me in forever. It's a haunting feeling wanting to get something back like that. My attitude would have been less moody about it if I had known those times were numbered. Oh, I miss those big bodacious hugs. If I could go back, I would squeeze her so tight, kneel down and look her in the eyes and tell her how awesome she made me feel doing that. How I would never, ever forget. She made me feel like the most important person in the world! I would tell her how absolutely radiant she is. How you could see her heart glowing because she loved you so big! Most importantly I'd tell her that I love her more than she would ever, ever know. Then with great joy hug her so tight and say to her that I was very proud to be her big sister, even if I never showed it. Oh, to hug her again. I hope I get to run to her and hug her so tight like she did to me in Dairy Queen. Who knows what we will get to do, but next to dancing with Jesus and worshiping God every day, I hope I get to run to her.

My hardest landmark is the bridge they found my sister by. That bridge is the bridge the bad man left my baby sister's dead body by. I had to go over that bridge for my graduation ceremony. I think I even considered taking a longer route or something. Which is ridiculous because you have to leave and go out and then around this other long way. But it crossed my mind. That bridge I thankfully don't have to travel when I go to see my best friend. When I do though it hurts a little. We stopped by there once. We got out and looked around. Searching for something, maybe Mom was searching for closure. That bridge is only two miles from where the murderer lived. It's why he chose it to leave her at. In the wooded area so that you can't see. There is no way anyone would have seen her. One of my best friends had a house there in a subdivision right behind it and I had to drive by there when I would visit for a few years, until they moved. Each time it hurts, but not as bad anymore. In fact now there is this cool drive-up restaurant for boats to dock, that's right across from where she was. My best friend's family and I go there every Summer for ice cream and drinks. I'm making good memories in that area because I don't want to be held captive by the bad. One day I'll show my kiddo's that just across the street was where my sister's body was found. I hope they ask me questions like, *why did you bring us here so close?* I want to tell them that I was set free a long time and that I had the choice of how I would deal with things. Momma decided to not be a prisoner. Besides, my best friend is here and we are only thirty minutes away and it's one of the coolest towns- so I'm gonna enjoy it!

This town is not bad for me, but there was no way to make it home after our tragedy. Too many people knew of our suffering and I didn't want to be gawked at. Seen as this poor soul who had a horrible mother and dead younger sister. When I visit that town it's not with a heavy heart but a free heart wrapped up in a few memory stings. I love bringing my kids here because it makes me feel a little like I can share more history of my kids Aunt that way. I've taken them to where she played softball. My goodness it does make me feel closer to her once again. I see her. I hear her laughing. The memories flood in so then I am there with her. In an instant. We are back in nineteen ninety-seven, back at the football field, we are back at the fast-food place I worked at. We are back anywhere in that town. My sister is there. As painful as it may feel, it is well with my soul too. Maybe coming back is a little sad but the overwhelming feeling of our life together is so much more worth it. I could sit on a patch of grass and close my eyes at the softball field and all I need is just a few breaths. The memories flood in. All five of us are still there. Our life wasn't bad, it was ours. Meek, busy, and sometimes hard, but we still had great times. My Mom did the best she could. I will never doubt that.

Memories

Many years have passed since those summer days.
Among the fields of barley.
See the children run as the sun goes down.
Among the fields of gold.
You'll remember me when the west wind moves.
Upon the fields of barley.
— Fields of Gold- Sting

There are memories that you truly cherish and then there are those that you wish you had a filter for before it became a memory. A memory I cherish, but also feel bad about was when my sister was a preschooler and I was a tween. We were in our bedroom cutting paper and I asked her to hold a piece while I cut the edge off. But then snip! I snipped off the edge of her thumb! We ran to the bathroom and I tried to stop the bleeding. Over the sink running the water over the cut I scolded her not to cry. After a few minutes when I knew we needed an adult, I reluctantly fetched Mom. She had to go to the ER and she didn't even tell the old people there that were asking what happened; that her big sister did it. Mom said she was so brave. She got a couple of stitches and she was such a tough cookie about it. Unlike her big sister who sat there with knots in my stomach and tears. These memories, though they are few, play in my head like movies sometimes. My heart sighs as I wish I could remember more. I'm thankful I do have the ones I do. Like the time I had to take her to get her softball pictures because Mom was working. When I picked her up she was already ready, but because I thought it would be cute, I made her take her ponytail out. She really didn't want to, she kinda gave me an attitude about it, but she did as I asked and we brushed her hair out and dropped her off. I regret that because Mom said she was really upset about that. Big scheme of things her hair was fine in a ponytail. It was just a softball picture anyway, not a glamor shot! One of my silly memories is of her and her best friend E. They would watch me dance. I love to dance. So many times I would dance in my room or while I cleaned and it made life feel better. It brought me joy. So I would dance to Enya or Sting, and sometimes Michael Jackson. They would watch and sometimes when I wasn't being a rude teenage brat; I would teach them to dance with me. My sister's best friend said to me that she and my sister looked up to me and wanted to be just like me. Ya know, it's a hard compliment to take since I could have been nicer to them instead of impatient. But, when I hear Field of Gold by Sting, I am there with those girls and we are dancing. We are friends and life is good. I just want to reach up to heaven and pull her down here with me. To dance. I can't wait to dance with her in heaven.

Then there are the times that I evoke my children to get the same response I would have from my youngest siblings. Like when you are driving in your car and you take one of those hilly bumps a little fast. It makes your tummy feel like it jumped and then the kids break out in laughter. My second daughter loves it! I look in my rearview mirror to recall that memory. Suddenly there I am, back in our town and they are in the back seat of my blue Honda. Laughing and grabbing bellies. We lived in a really hilly area and if I didn't need to stop at our house first I would pass it up and keep driving to Memaw's. There was a big hill right in front of our house and I would take it fast and my siblings would laugh so hard. The giggling would engulf us. I would watch them in the rearview and they would be giggling and grabbing their tummies. I love it. So I love doing it to my own children. And my sister is there.

I remember little everyday things. Her little sayings she would copy from shows we watched. Her chasing our potbelly pig around and laughing because it was so hard to get that pig to stay where we put it. My mom used to warm up her and my brother's clothes in the morning in the dryer because it was so cold in the house in the morning. Well, one time my kitten climbed in there and basically was killed by accident. My sister was so sorrowful with me. She tried so hard to console me and I was moved by her heart for me during something so sad.

One Christmas I woke up early to peek out my door to catch a glimpse of what was under the tree. I never left my room but I scanned to see what Santa had brought, because in our home those were the unwrapped toys. There was a bike- I thought for sure it was mine. Turned out to be my sister's though, even if it felt disappointing for me she was cute about her new bike. Therefore, I decided to be happy about it with her.

When we first moved close to the ocean, my grandmother would take us all fishing. But a few times we went fishing near the ocean. The whole clan would do this together, so it was cousins and all. Grandma would tie a chicken leg on the end of a string to catch crabs. The youngest would wade with theirs in the shallow end, dragging it back and forth calling out "Here fishy, fishy!" Oh my word, we would laugh until we cried. The irony of calling your food, whilst walking in the water that the said crab would be in. Such a sweet memory.

One of my memories that was not great was the night she asked me to stay the night. She is standing there the night before she was murdered. Begging me to stay the night. I lived with my Memaw and so sometimes she wanted to stay too. But it was a school night and I said no. I had to study for a test, and I was looking forward to talking to a new boy on the phone. I'm sure I was annoyed when I told her no. I'm sure I hurt her feelings, and I hate that now. That was the last time I saw her alive. Me telling her no. I wish I had told her yes; with every beat of my heart I wish I had said yes. She would still be here. Here to annoy me and love me. I know the gravity of this thought. I have had it a thousand times. I'm grateful that Jesus redeemed me. I didn't fall for Satan's lie that would have filled me with guilt. Maybe stolen my life.

He Saved Me

Jesus, Jesus
Let me tell you how I feel.
You have given me your Spirit
I love you so.
– Walk to Emmaus song

Truth is I can't fathom a day without Jesus. Can't imagine my life without Him. Daily I'm thinking about Him and his abundant love and grace and how unconditional it truly is. Most of my decisions are heaven bound, and yet I am a pitiful sinner. I sin in the most gut-wrenching ways because my Redemption doesn't make me immune to the most basic pitfalls. Which then I have the terrible habit of beating myself up over because I should know better. Right? My experience with great tragedy should help me handle things differently, but I am human even if I wish it weren't so. There are so many days when I choose not to give my children sufficient grace or I strain my sibling relationships because of my high expectations. And many, many times I forget to not worry. I read Matthew 6:19-24 from time to time. It basically tells us that God even cares for the birds, but I let the earthly worry appear and when it does He gently reminds me to remember the birds. Thank goodness the morning brings new everything.

One of the most impactful messages I remember hearing early on was by a man in Amway. Like with any MLM, they have books and CD's that they recommend you read and listen to. One of those CD's was done by a man and he was speaking at a Leadership about choosing life. His teaching was about how your words and actions contribute to whether you want to live life or death. But it's more about the subtle ways you can choose life. Like how God tells us to in the Bible, Deuteronomy 30:15 See, I set before you today life and prosperity, death and destruction. There is so much in the Bible that begs us to choose life and turn from death. Death means more to me than just the actual dying of your body and returning to the ground. It means those everyday words you say or thoughts and definitely your actions. That CD made such an impact on me that if I am making a choice outside of what I want, I'm still convicted enough about it to turn it around. That message to this day, eighteen years later, is still something I understand to live by. Be encouraging. Pray healing over myself, children, and friends. Be positive, dream in this life, focus on the good and most importantly **BE** the good.

My sweet friend, whose name is spelled like my sisters; loves to remind me that I have a beautiful life. And she's right, I do have a beautiful life. It's been a ride to get here but it's glorious. I made up my mind years ago that I didn't want to stay the same. I wanted to grow and stretch myself a little. I wanted for someone who hadn't seen me in years to meet me again and see a different girl. I wanted to make my sister proud. All that growth is credit to reading my Bible, leadership and Christian books and going outside my comfort zone. During this time was part of my healing time.

Before my recent divorce my heart was set on being in the

Women's Ministry. Serving makes me feel alive. Very well like I am in my gift that God made me for. Something about feeling so alone sometimes or even overwhelmed and then you serve others and it feels like home. I remember the first time it clicked for me and it even felt a little like my sister was there. Smiling. I felt like because of my path, it makes me want to help others and God knows that. I can tell Him every day that I am not enough, yet that is my reminder of why ministry is so important. There are plenty of tired people who think that same thing. *I am not enough. I don't have enough.* It's insane to go on in life to feel like that or think like that. It's a good devil lie. But also, everyone feels the weight of the world in different ways. I don't think I would have ever dreamed of serving in this way. When I am serving, whether it be in the church's nursery or greeting sweet families, or behind the scenes- I feel her there. Smiling. Like she knows I am happy. Truth is, the divorce may have made me feel less equipped to lead women, but I've never felt like God wouldn't use me in other ways. Once I picked myself up with God's help I knew that He would STILL use me for his works. I wasn't forsaken. Still.

I'm excited because I still have all this life to live. To dream about all the things I can do with my life. Anticipating where God will lead me. There is so much hope. Hope is a life giver. It's fresh air and wings. When my sister was murdered, even in my darkness there was a desire to do good for others. I thought that meant becoming a family law Judge or something. The word purpose had a new meaning. Little did I know that being a light on the hill is a great purpose. ***It's enough.*** My season right now is tough work. I am in the thick of being a single mom with four kiddos. I'm no longer in the comfort of being financially dependent on someone else so I am a full-time working mother. Recently I purchased a car by myself, secured a corporate job and am qualified to buy a home. All by the grace of God. I've been praying like no one's business my friend. Without ceasing. I'm not discouraged by the season I am in. I's here and I better make the best of it!! There will be a new one that has new perks or new heartaches. Maybe even life changing events will occur. I'm not discouraged. Just give me Jesus. One day, just maybe I *will* be in the Women's Ministry. I dream so that I keep choosing life. I dream so that my kids know what it looks like. I have hope. I owe my whole life, everything I have to my Heavenly Father and the one who hung on the cross for me. I owe it all. So I chose life. If I could look you in the eyes and tell you one thing … it'd be that I found everything I needed when I read the Bible. Everything. And kiddo's…never stop talking to Jesus. We have a friend in Jesus and no one loves you more than God, and **absolutely** the Holy Spirit will guide you. I hope that I have shown you with it looks like to rely on God. To stand firm. To be a light. To be madly in love with God.

Acknowledgments

Mom…I'm incredibly proud of you. Look what you did after the world try to steal your life. You took it back. Thank you for being my ride or die.

Cindy and Kathy…thank you for gently leading me to Jesus.

My best friend since I was sixteen…thank you for being home to me.

My family redeemer Mr. James…where would I be without you?

My Irish twin…I love you. I hope you always choose to dance.

My little brother… I will always root for you.

My platinum hair beauty…I could never repay you.

My in-laws… thank you for taking in a girl who didn't know God and loving me through it all. Showing me what a faith filled family looks like. I'm grateful.

Friend… you will always be my sister's best friend.